"Homeschooling is one of the most important reform movements in America today. And now Linda Dobson has revealed to a wider audience the secrets of its success. This inspired and inspiring guide is a terrific introduction to why homeschooling works and how the rest of us can learn its many lessons. If you want to bring out the best in your children—and in our society—here's your homework: Read this book!"

—DANIEL H. PINK, author,
Free Agent Nation

"This book is a revelation. It corrects the misunderstandings that surround the growing number of children being educated at home and turns them into something special. As Linda Dobson makes clear, it is the rest of us who can learn much from the homeschoolers as we guide our children through regular schools. I was particularly impressed by the sense of fun and exploration that goes into the best of homeschooling lessons."

—JAY MATHEWS
Washington Post Education Reporter

"Contrary to popular misconception, homeschooling is more about parents helping children live and learn in their communities than it is about sheltering them at home. As Linda Dobson so eloquently explains, that opportunity isn't closed to schooled children. She provides hundreds of exciting ideas and useful tips for accessing the numerous real-life learning opportunities that exist outside of classrooms and textbooks. Aside from any "academic edge" that can result, Dobson's instructions for learning from life are bound to nurture children's personal growth while increasing their self-esteem and creative thinking abilities."

—WENDY PRIESNITZ, editor
Life Learning Magazine

What the Rest of Us Can Learn from Homeschooling

How A+ Parents Can Give Their Traditionally Schooled Kids the Academic Edge

LINDA DOBSON

THREE RIVERS PRESS

NEW YORK

Published by Three Rivers Press, New York, New York.
Member of the Crown Publishing Group, a division of Random House, Inc.
www.randomhouse.com

THREE RIVERS PRESS and the Tugboat design are registered trademarks of Random House, Inc.

Printed in the United States of America

Library of Congress Cataloging-in-Publication Data
Dobson, Linda.
    What the rest of us can learn from homeschooling : how A+ parents can give their traditionally schooled kids the academic edge / Linda Dobson.— 1st ed.
        p.   cm.
    Includes index.
    ISBN 0-7615-1977-7
    1. Education—Parent participation—United States. 2. Home schooling—United States. I. Title.
    LB1048.5 .D617 2003
    371.04'2—dc21   2003007242

ISBN 0-7615-1977-7

10 9 8 7 6 5 4 3 2

First Edition

For Susie and Serena,
my newest teachers,
who arrived as a set

and

With thanks to Jamie Miller
a gifted and dedicated editor,
who through the years
became much more, a
cherished friend

Contents

PART FOUR

Focus On: Your Important Role   189

Introduction

As I begin work on this book, leaves rapidly falling from the trees swirl in wind gusts, delivering the unmistakable scent of autumn. Yet the monster marigolds outside my large picture window remain amazingly vibrant, attracting a monarch butterfly slowly flitting from flower to flower. I pause to watch.

What a wonderful vision to introduce a discourse on the practices and lessons that homeschooling families have gleaned as they learn at home with their children. That gorgeous black and orange creature appears to go about its innate goal in a random, almost haphazard fashion. We understand, though, through our experience and observation of many butterflies over the years, that it is doing what comes naturally, seeking what it needs when it needs it, perfectly capable of surviving just as it should.

Many of the homeschooling children I have met over the last eighteen years go about learning and living in much the same way. Indeed, compared to the order and regulation of public schooling with which most of us are familiar, a homeschooling child's education often appears to unfold in a manner as random as the butterfly's. Yet those who live with and observe these children have come to understand there is order in the chaos. It's just that the order is dictated to a great extent by the children's needs and interests rather than by a somewhat arbitrary school schedule and curriculum.

Viewed this way, homeschooling is really a surprisingly simple concept, if only we (a) accept that each child is different; developing at her own rate intellectually, emotionally, psychologically, and spiritually; and dreaming dreams unique to her experience and innermost calling and (b) open our minds to the possibility that the commonly accepted school schedule and curriculum as *the* way to learn isn't the only way, and may not even be the best way for all of those uniquely different children.

The good news is that if you can accept part (a), it's relatively easy to wrap your mind around part (b), that the school schedule and curriculum may not be the best way for all children to learn. As you read this book, try to keep in mind this fundamental distinction made by homeschooling families and think in terms of how you can apply it to your own family. The important thing to remember is that the order of education is dictated by the child's needs and interests rather than by a rigid school schedule and curriculum.

For a previous book titled *Homeschoolers' Success Stories,* I had the privilege of interviewing two dozen adults who were homeschooled. These folks were successful whether their families used a curriculum or not. They succeeded if their families were rich or poor. Success occurred regardless of the families' reasons for homeschooling. Indeed, there were only two threads common to their diverse experiences:

- they used as much time as possible to learn about and participate in topics of personal interest

- they received understanding, help, and advocacy from parents or other significant adults

Homeschoolers' success rests on two priorities: giving the child as much freedom of time as possible and giving the child as much adult support as possible. This is the learning lifestyle, and it's where our journey into the secrets of homeschooling families will begin. Think of it as the foundation upon which all your activity will build. Next, we'll consider your child as the unique learner she is before focusing on creating a favorable learning environment. Last but certainly not least important, we'll spotlight the extremely important role you play, from allowing your child to witness your own learning mistakes and victories to helping out with her schoolwork.

In this book, I warmly invite you to take a good look at how homeschoolers experience education. Begin to imagine what life would be like if, when it comes to your children's education, it occurs in a way that best serves *their* needs, goals, and dreams.

May the learning road rise up to meet you.

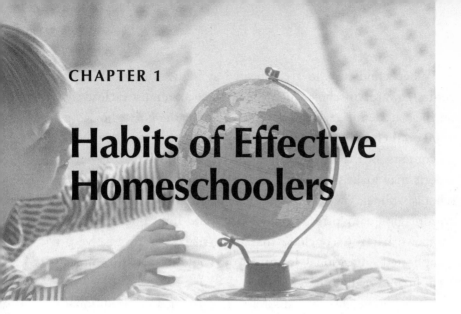

CHAPTER 1

Habits of Effective Homeschoolers

"True openness means closedness to all the charms that make us comfortable with the present."

ALLAN BLOOM, *The Closing of the American Mind*

A S A LITTLE BOY, David Beihl enjoyed learning about state capitals. When he and his mom discovered the existence of the National Geography Bee, they thought it might be fun for him to enter someday. Five years later, David had entered—not once but four times. In the last year he was eligible, David finally won first place, a $25,000 scholarship, and a family trip to Australia.

"I think my parents helped me study better," David told me. "They helped me find ways to study that worked for me. Even if you have the world's best teachers, they can't work with twenty or thirty children in a way that makes the best use of their different styles of learning."

When children who are educated at home win yet another contest, award, or scholarship, the media focus almost exclusively on their academic excellence. We read about the girls who score 1600 on their SATs, the homeschooled teams that win the robotics contests, or the boy who wins the citywide spelling bee. Such reports may make parents who send their children to traditional schools wonder, "What are these families doing that we're not?" You imagine daily drills, weekly exams, and hour upon hour of "homework." You conclude that their success must involve a complicated educational formula you couldn't possibly implement in your own home.

Some homeschooled children's lives do include traditional school elements: textbooks, tests, grades, book reports, and everything else you remember from your own school experience. Other homeschoolers who win titles, however, awake each morning to activity bearing as little resemblance to school as a trip in a Lear jet approximates a trek in a covered wagon. This is the first clue that more lies at the heart of homeschoolers' educational success than pencils and books.

Because reporters don't ask the right questions, you'll never find vital answers in the media about why or how parents like you and me become the A+ parents who provide their children with an academic edge. You might never realize that you can do the same no matter how much money or education you have, where you live, or how old your child is. If you're looking for ways to improve your child's self-esteem, responsibility, and outlook on life, as well as her grades, you've come to the right place.

In this book, we'll examine the four major components that come together to enhance your child's sense of wonder and interest in the world to create a successful, happy learning experience for your entire family. First, we'll focus on creating what is called "the learning lifestyle" through which education becomes a priority incorporated into everyday life. Choose a few of the ways to catch the learning lifestyle attitude, learn about the power of your parental love, use the hints to make more time together, and start thinking "outside the box."

Second, we'll focus on your child as a unique learner. You will see the reasons to put the "child" back into childhood, discover how easy it is to figure out his learning style and innate intelligences and how to use them to his advantage, and bring to light the six principles of successful learning for every child.

Third, we'll focus on creating a favorable learning environment with the concept of "flow" as your guide to enrich and expand your child's educational experience. Grab your walking shoes, because you're soon going to take advantage of your community, a child's best classroom.

Finally, we'll explore your very important role in your academically (and otherwise!) successful child's life. You'll find the job of learning facilitator may be much more appealing than the thought of becoming another of your child's teachers. Learn how to exercise your child's basic learning skills as you go about daily life by doing nothing more than "thinking out loud." Become an ally in tackling homework—and study and organizational skills—before realizing just how much you discover about yourself and the world as you help your child.

7 Habits of Successful Homeschoolers

We create habits when we engage in an activity so long and so often that we begin to do it without even thinking about it. While some habits are bad (like skipping breakfast) and others annoying (like strumming fingers on the table), many are good (like saying please and thank you). Like many other good habits, we first had to learn what polite behavior is, and then practice it repeatedly, in order to become habitually polite people.

The same notion applies to becoming an A+ parent. Activities that lead us in that direction become so well established that our inclination to perform them is often unconscious and effortless. Like saying thank you, we perform such activities without a second thought.

The following habits are those that many effective homeschoolers use to create the foundation upon which they build a happy, successful educational experience with their children. If you make a point of practicing them repeatedly, one day soon they'll come as naturally as saying thank you. And just as the act of saying thank you has become an integral aspect of your life, so, too, will the act of automatically performing the following habits become an integral aspect of your life as an A+ parent.

HABIT 1: TRUSTING IN YOURSELF AND YOUR CHILD

John Holt, often credited as the "granddaddy of homeschooling," in his landmark book *How Children Learn* (Dell, 1967), boiled down the complicated business of helping children learn into just two words: "Trust children." This sounds so simple, but in our culture it just may be the hardest task to accomplish. Why? Holt explained it's difficult "because to trust children we must first learn to trust ourselves, and most of us were taught as children that we could not be trusted."

This may explain our willingness to rely on the advice of experts in many areas of life, including education. While in some cases their advice does make the initial trouble go away, what are the consequences when we relinquish responsibility this way?

"Relying on 'experts' to solve our problems leaves us feeling even more dependent on others, less self-assured of our ability to manage our own lives, and more likely to run to yet another 'expert' in the future," I wrote in *The Art of Education: Reclaiming Your Family, Community, and Self* (Holt Associates, revised 1997). "Our immediate problem has vanished, but the side effects of dependency never go away." Under such conditions we can become alienated from our own feelings, thoughts, and choices.

When we take responsibility instead of relegating it to an expert, we get back in touch with those feelings and thoughts that are unique to our situation and unavailable to outside experts. Before long, we can increase trust in ourselves and the choices we make.

A basic habit of A+ parents, then, is trust in oneself, in the validity of our thoughts and feelings and in our ability to make choices and take intelligent action accordingly. When it comes to our children, who has the most current and intimately informed connection? It's we parents, of course. And aren't up-to-date and well-informed folks in any field called "experts"?

As your child's parent, trust that you possess the love and wisdom necessary to provide whatever help he needs in his ongoing flight toward independence. When you reclaim your natural gifts in this regard, you will find it easier to trust your children. You will trust that they contain within them the seed of desire to learn, and you will begin to see your role as that of a learning guide, much like a gardener whose job it is to help that seed grow.

A gardener knows she cannot force a seed to grow. She cannot make a marigold seed blossom into a rose. She cannot change the seed in any fundamental way. Instead, she protects the young seed from potentially harmful conditions that through her experience she knows can limit growth. She nourishes it and creates an environment that encourages the seed to reach its full potential. She accepts that all the seeds in her garden will not sprout on the same day, nor will they all blossom on the same day, nor will they wind up with an equal number of flowers. Doing all that she can to help, at the same time she trusts the nature of the seeds to grow.

You can help your child excel by trusting the innate, natural human tendency to grow and learn, and then creating an environment that will best support this. (There is much more about learning environment to come in part three.) Once you develop the habit of trust in yourself and your child, you'll find it easier to reclaim responsibility for your child's education.

HABIT 2: KEEPING ALIVE THE JOY OF LEARNING

A preschool child in a new environment is a wondrous sight to behold. Her eyes light up as each new stimulus turns the ever-burning spark of her intrinsic curiosity into fire. All that natural child energy rises to serve her as she plunges into exploration, moving from one discovery to the next in perpetual motion as she feeds an insatiable hunger for meaning and connection. She is nothing short of a little learning machine.

Fast-forward to your child's school years. In a paper he wrote, Nicholas H. Apostoleris asks, "Is a declining love of learning as children grow developmentally appropriate and inevitable? Are the learning environments a factor? Is it love of learning which is waning, or is it a love of the subjects taught in school?" The paper is available online at www.alphadevelopmental.com/dissertation.pdf. (To give away the answers, they are no, yes, and the latter.)

A useful habit is to do everything possible to keep your child's love of learning alive or rekindle it if something, usually a series of unpleasant learning experiences, has extinguished it. Rick Martin, a teenager in a Seattle suburb, knows why his parents saw a change in him after he attended kindergarten. "I was being forced to learn in school, and quickly turning away from wanting to learn," he recalls. "By the end of the year I wouldn't complete the art projects I loved at the beginning of the year. Pure and simple, I was becoming depressed with school," Rick realizes.

His mom, Janine, knew Rick as energetic and strong-willed and saw the very qualities she loved about her child slipping away. "In order for Rick to get reenergized, I knew I had to give him as much free rein, educationally speaking, as possible," says Janine. "So when he got home from school, I made sure his time was his. I knew he felt as if his beloved art had been 'stolen' from him at school, so I purchased more drawing materials and left them on the coffee table. After a few weeks I saw him doodling again," Janine remembers. "Within two months he was painting up a storm again, as well as reading about twenty books each week—no kidding! He was glad to do it 'his way,' and I was just thrilled to have my little boy back."

HABIT 3: DEFINING EDUCATION FOR YOUR OWN FAMILY

Your child will invest a minimum of thirteen years getting her education, so why not make sure it's your agenda that guides it—your family values, your hopes and dreams, your take on what it's important to know—by getting into the habit of defining it yourself.

Your definition of education will serve as a road map as you and your family travel down the learning lifestyle road together. It will help guide your many decisions, saving you the time, money, and energy you could waste rambling down an educational dead end.

Carrie Morgan faced a dilemma that could happen to any learning lifestyle family. She was homeschooling two children and felt very unsure of what she was doing. When Carrie spoke to one parent, she loved the idea of what that family was doing so much she ran out and bought everything necessary to do the same. "Then I'd talk to another family and find out they were learning all about ancient Rome, and I'd drop everything else to do that because *that* was important for my children to know," Carrie remembers. "Then my next door neighbor would innocently ask if my older child was reading yet, and I'd torture my poor little guy with six hours of phonics. It was like every time the wind shifted we'd blow in another direction until one day I decided that I needed to figure out exactly what it was I was trying to accomplish so I could accomplish it!"

Carrie spent several weeks pondering what constitutes a well-educated person. She wrote several pages, edited them, and then wrote some more until her definition was brief enough to hang on her refrigerator door where she could see it every day. Carrie felt an educated person would have, among other things, a deep and wide knowledge base to draw from and love learning enough to continue doing it throughout his lifetime. He would be able to communicate effectively, know how to find whatever information he might need, read well, and be math-savvy enough to at least take care of daily needs (with the hope for enough fascination to learn of math's connection to the workings of the universe).

"Having my list allowed me to focus our time, attention, and resources where they were most needed to accomplish these goals," says Carrie. "It allowed me to put all the neat things other families were doing into perspective and to keep them in their proper place in 'the big picture.' I can't tell you how much stress this relieved—it was liberating!"

Your definition need not be long or terribly fancy—in fact, the more succinct, the better. It should be honest; and don't worry if it doesn't agree with what you understand your child's school's goals to be. It should begin with the desired end in mind. And it should be flexible so that when you revisit it now and again after you begin living the learning lifestyle (see chapter 2) you may incorporate your inevitable new wisdom about learning—and yourselves—into it.

HABIT 4: FOCUSING ON LEARNING, NOT TEACHING

A key to effective learning, say homeschoolers, is to habitually focus on helping your child learn. This is because there is a world of difference between the act of teaching a child and the act of assisting his learning process.

"Children don't need to be 'taught' as much as they need a rich environment with tools and opportunities to learn," says Lillian Jones, who began homeschooling her now grown son, Ethan, when he was seven years old. "We all learn in different ways," she explains, "and we are the ones who instinctively know the most

JUST ENJOY

Get some of those great books from the library or bookstore on kids' fun science experiments, and do them with your kids. Don't even think about quizzing them on what they're learning; just let them have fun and learn whatever they learn. The main thing they'll be learning is how much fun learning can be.

Lead them in relaxing and enjoying life. Toast marshmallows for no reason, read poetry aloud, make real hot chocolate from scratch—create memories. Extending an already long school day isn't going to make your child a better learner but enhancing the quality of her experience of life will. I shudder to hear that people have passed on taking their kids on an interesting trip for a few days because they might "miss something" in school. What on earth could they miss in the course of a few days? I'll tell you what—the joy and fascination of new places and experiences they could have had on that trip! There's a big, fascinating world out there, and all too few kids get a chance to take it all in. The most important part of homeschooling for us was being together as a family and exploring our interests together out in the real world. This can be done whether or not a child is attending school.

Lillian Jones, Sebastapol, California

about our own methods of learning." (See a collection of Lillian's favorite articles on this subject at www.besthomeschooling.org.)

Carrie Morgan cultivated this habit at the same time she put together and began living her own definition of education. "I realized that almost everything on my list was much more a matter of appreciating and using what one learned than it was a matter of what one could be taught," she says. "Learning something, that act of discovery, allows my children to claim it as their own, a powerful incentive to keep going and really hone the skills they value.

"For example," Carrie continues, "one day, when he said he had nothing to do, my son saw the book on volcanoes I had picked up from the library and he leafed through it. He was fascinated by the 'mountains with fire coming out of them,' immediately went on the Internet to find out more, and was still looking for more information months later. If I had sat down and 'taught' my son all the scientific facts about volcanoes in the dry and dull manner textbooks are noted for," she says, "he probably would have yawned and forgotten about them as soon as we moved on to earthquakes."

When you cultivate the habit of focusing on learning, thoughts about "teaching" fall by the wayside. Although it may be tempting at first, you'll soon find little, if any, need to do an impression of ol' Mrs. Bunson, every second grader's nightmare, in your living room. The focus on learning eliminates much of the insecurity parents feel about their ability to assist their children's academic progress, because it doesn't require any special knowledge or training. Indeed, upon closer examination, what at first appear as selfless, sacrificial lives of homeschooling parents are merely lives where the families move ahead by assisting their children's learning process.

Does this all sound rather simple? Good, because it really is.

HABIT 5: UNLEARNING

Even if you haven't specifically studied education, you've learned a lot about learning over the years. Remember how we create a habit by engaging in an activity so long and so often that we begin to do it automatically? Well, the way we parents think about learning has become, for the most part, a habit.

In order to approach education differently, you will find you need to *think* about it differently. This may take a conscious effort to break the old habit to make room for the new. The fastest

THE TEACHER UNLEARNS

When I began homeschooling, even though I was a "teacher" I didn't have visions of "teaching" my children as I had taught in a classroom. I had done enough reading and had spoken to enough people to know that this approach would not work in our family. I felt challenged as I had to reexamine many of the beliefs I had adopted about learning and keep only those that supported the growth of the children and our family.

This is an ongoing process. I had to let go of the belief that the only way my children could learn was by me directing their learning. Being a "teacher" at this time was something I had to "un"learn. Whenever I tried "teaching," my children would tolerate it for a short while, and then it became too strenuous. I would remember a professor whom I really admired in my teacher education. He would say, "Learning should be like 'licking honey from a slate." I then would stop and let go of my control of how they were supposed to learn.

Sandra Strauss, Burlington, Ontario, Canada

path to stop thinking in the old way is to do away with, or *unlearn*, some of the ideas that fuel it.

For example, "I had to stop telling my two daughters to 'look it up,'" remembers Shay Seaborne, founder and moderator of VaEclecticHomeschool, an e-mail discussion list, from Woodbridge, Virginia. "It doesn't make sense not to share the answer if you know it. Making kids look it up can generate resentment and resistance to looking things up later in life." However, this only happened when Shay slipped into "teaching mode."

"Rather than trying to bestow knowledge upon them," says Shay, "my children strongly prefer that I simply share my interests and enthusiasm. It is when I am genuine, not consciously trying to instruct, that they are receptive to the experience."

If you ask one hundred home educators the most important thing they unlearned, you'll get one hundred different answers. Sandra Strauss learns at home in Ontario, Canada with her husband and three children. This former teacher works part-time finding families to serve as hosts for international students visiting Canada for exposure to English and the Canadian multicultural experience. "I had to let go of the belief that children, when left to do what interests them, will do nothing valuable," Sandra recalls. "Now I know children can and should do what they want. My role has become helping them get and do what they want in life. It turns out the best thing I can do for them is stay out of their way! I ask for their input, answer questions, and give my opinion when I'm asked and, at times, when I'm not asked."

Cultivate the habit of unlearning and turning ideas about education upside down and inside out. This will lead you to some of the best learning about learning you'll ever find.

HABIT 6: STAYING ON TOP OF EDUCATIONAL ISSUES

Most homeschooling parents are "on top" of educational issues. While other moms may peruse *Reader's Digest,* many a homeschooling mom reads *Education Week* instead. When you realize you shoulder the responsibility for your child's education, you need to know which methods and theories are supported by replicable scientific research and which are simply the educational fad of the month.

"Many homeschoolers don't have the time or money to waste on what doesn't work," says Kay Brooks, founder of TnHomeEd.com, a network and comprehensive information clearinghouse for Tennessee homeschoolers. "So we do our research. Your child may only have one chance to get the basics right. Don't let others waste that opportunity."

EDUCATION NEWS SOURCES

Education Gadfly: weekly on the Web from Thomas B. Fordham
    Foundation: www.edexcellence.net./gadfly

Education Info: randomly received e-mail with information from and about
    U.S. Department of Education publications. To subscribe, address an
    e-mail message to: listproc@inet.ed.gov. Then write SUBSCRIBE EDIN-
    FO YOURFIRSTNAME YOURLASTNAME in the message

Education Intelligence Agency Communique: weekly e-mail report on
    teachers' union activity. Sign up on the Web at www.eiaonline.com

EdNetBriefs: weekly (during school year) synopsis via e-mail:
    www.edbriefs.com/sub.html

 or on the Web: www.edbriefs.com

Education News: daily e-mail with links to actual articles around the
    globe: www.EducationNews.org

Education Week: weekly on the Web: www.edweek.org

Ed Watch: online publication of the Maple River Education Coalition:
    www.edwatch.org

"No Child Left Behind" Final Regulations:
    www.ed.gov/PressReleases/11-2002/11262002.html

School News Monitor: top-ten stories of the week at
    www.eiaonline.com/monitor.htm

School Reform News: free subscription at www.heartland.org

A mother of four in Nashville who began homeschooling ten
years ago, Kay offers some concrete suggestions. "Homeschoolers
buy books about homeschooling, but public school parents rarely

buy books about public education, and even more rarely do they buy books critical of the system," she says. "It's important for your child that you do your homework, too."

Local Level

There are many levels on which to keep up. You can find out a lot about your local school system by networking with other parents and keeping each other informed. Your child's teacher should be able to provide you with a copy of her curriculum. This document outlines the plan for the entire school year and sets forth the order in which topics will be covered. Think of it as the classroom's agenda, setting the tone and procedure for the year just as an agenda does for a meeting. Call or meet with the teacher to get a sense of the timing of coverage—before Christmas? Right after spring break? Just prior to the end of the year?

With a few pieces of paper and pen at hand, review the curriculum. On one sheet, jot down every immediate idea you have about how you may either enhance a topic or help your child learn it in a different way. For example, if you discover your child's class will study the Civil War and your parents live just outside Gettsyburg, Pennsylvania, you can plan a relevant field trip. Write it down. If you read that your child will be taught about India for social studies, you make a note that watching the *Gandhi* video could add meaning to the study.

Use another sheet of paper to take notes about things you have to look up. For instance, if your child will study percentages and fractions this year, what software might you buy for your home computer to help make the study more fun? If science includes a study of climate and weather, might the retired meteorologist down the street like to come for dinner that week? Didn't you once see a science kit on climate in the toy store? Would it be a timely Christmas or birthday gift? Might the library be planning to have a speaker address that or a related subject?

Review the curriculum with your child. Explain what the contents mean, especially if the curriculum is written, as many are, in "educationese." Encourage her to be frank about all the topics. Ask for her ideas on how to enhance her study. Likely she'll know about even more software and movies, books, and community members and what they have to offer.

Perhaps she'll groan when she sees she'll be studying weather—maybe you shouldn't waste your money on that kit you were thinking about. On the other hand, discovering she'll also study simple machines may make her eyes light up. Maybe the toy store—or the science store—or an online store—sells kits that contain everything you need to make your own clock. On yet another sheet of paper write down your child's suggestions and note those that may need further research. It shouldn't be difficult to rally your child's research help when he finds the topic interesting. If he doesn't know how to conduct research, working together is a real-life way to get him started.

State Level

Because educational decisions are made at the state level, it's important to keep in touch with your state representatives and to stay informed about what they may have planned. Every state maintains a Web site where it announces new bills. By making a quick phone call, you can find out when an issue is scheduled for discussion, and you can plan to attend. "Homeschoolers are famous for their ability to put a fine point on the issue and let their legislators know what they want," explains Kay. "Be politically active." Election years bring many chances to meet your candidates, and it's easy to arrange an informal meeting with a group of parents at the school, a local church, or in your own living room.

National Level

Kay Brooks worries that organizations such as the National Education Association (NEA), the American Federation of Teachers

(AFT), and the Parents Teachers Association (PTA) are most often lobbyists on school issues. When an issue warrants the attention of these or similar organizations, it's important to understand the organization's position and why. Armed with such crucial information, you'll be better prepared to judge if that position best serves your child's interests.

HABIT 7: JUMPING IN, MAKING MISTAKES

In 1921, as a sloppy health clinician prepared a batch of yummy bran gruel, he spilled some directly onto the stovetop where it rapidly sizzled into a crisp flake. As brave as he was curious, the clinician took a bite and found it tasty. Thanks to this accident, we enjoy Wheaties cereal today. Indeed, many great inventions had similarly inauspicious beginnings, commonly called mistakes.

Somewhere along the line, mistakes got a bad rap they don't really deserve. (Probably as a result of them being terrible reminders of school, but I digress.) Not only are mistakes a fact of life, they are a source of fabulous learning opportunities. As William James once said, "Without mistakes, how would we know what we have to work on?"

This holds true for your children, and we'll cover that in more depth shortly. Right now we're talking about *you* as you learn how to learn with your children. Get in the habit of jumping in and making mistakes. Contrary to much of the media hype, homeschoolers are real families with real parents who sometimes lose their tempers or wish they could just stay in bed all day. They live with real children who sometimes don't want to walk the dog or eat their vegetables. They make a lot of mistakes others don't necessarily see, yet most acknowledge that some of their own best learning occurs as a result.

An important aspect of the mistakes you'll make is your ability to admit them to your children. Maria Romano is a New Jersey mom with four children in public school. Her eldest, Sophie, had a long history of school problems, from not doing homework to frequent detention for sassing a teacher. One day, the school secretary called Maria at work to inform her that Sophie had started a fight with another girl, was being suspended, and needed a ride home.

"I was so angry with Sophie I couldn't see straight," Maria remembers. "When I picked her up I didn't even ask if she was hurt. She'd been threatened with suspension for any more problems, and here we were."

"I didn't start it," Sophie said softly on the ride home.

"I told her I didn't believe her," Maria says, "and I didn't believe her the next dozen times she claimed that, either."

Two days into Sophie's suspension, Maria received another call at work. This time it was the school principal. "The other girl just came in with her mother and confessed that her friends had egged her on to fight with Sophie. I'm sorry, Mrs. Romano," said the principal. "Sophie can return to school tomorrow."

Maria called home to give Sophie the good news and, more important, to apologize for not believing her. "Discipline has always been pretty strict in our home, and telling Sophie I'd made a mistake was one of the hardest things I've ever done."

When Maria returned home from work she went to Sophie's room where she saw several packed suitcases. "What in the world is going on?" Maria asked.

"I was on my way to the bus station," said Sophie. "If you hadn't called to tell me you were wrong, that you'd made a mistake, I would have been gone by now."

Like Maria, you'll be a bigger person for admitting mistakes and do much to strengthen or, as in Maria's case, save your relationship with your child. Everyone appreciates honesty. An added bonus is seeing your child understand that it's more important to make the attempt than it is to be right, a very useful habit throughout life. You'll provide a living example, more powerful than words, that learning is a lifelong opportunity that continues long after one has left school. And who knows? While habitually

HABITS OF EFFECTIVE HOMESCHOOLERS

- Reclaim as much responsibility for your child's education as you possibly can

- Keep alive—or rekindle—the joy of learning that once permeated your child's discoveries

- Define education, with your child if appropriate, for your own family

- Focus on learning, and your need to be "teacher" will disappear

- Unlearn just as much about education as you learn

- Stay on top of educational issues at the local, state, and national levels

- Jump in, make mistakes

jumping in and making mistakes, one of you may end up inventing the next cereal sensation to sweep the nation.

Now that you're cultivating these habits, let's dig a bit deeper into how you, too, can catch the learning lifestyle attitude.

PART ONE

Focus on:
Lifestyle

"Something we were withholding made us weak
Until we found it was ourselves."

ROBERT FROST, *"The Gift Outright," 1942*

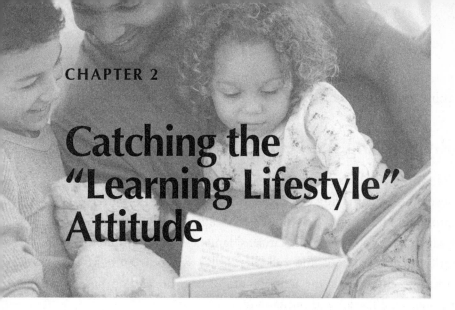

CHAPTER 2

Catching the "Learning Lifestyle" Attitude

OUR DIVERSE NATION is home to many different life-styles. One family lives simply while next door a country gentleman enjoys the lifestyle of the rich. Somewhere in the same neighborhood are people living gay, religious, or feminist lifestyles.

What is it that defines and determines a lifestyle? Simply, it's the underlying philosophy, the navigational light, if you will, that guides our major life decisions. Lifestyle arises from the core of our individual beliefs, the beliefs that receive first consideration in all our life choices.

We make our lifestyle visible to others by where we choose to live, how we spend (or don't spend) our money, and why we gravitate to some folks as friends and not others. Our lifestyle becomes apparent through the political candidates we vote for, the charities we support, and the subjects we like to discuss in conversation. A very important indicator of lifestyle is how we fill our nonwork hours, that time available for freely chosen activities. In short, our lifestyle comes about from the values we think are most important.

Reinventing the Learning Lifestyle

Requiring compulsory attendance at a public school is a relatively recent concept, having only been around for about 150 years (its proponents originally envisioned schooling lasting only the few years it then took to ensure citizens' language and math literacy). Prior to this, what we now call "life skills" were transmitted from adults to children via the activities of everyday life and purposeful apprenticeships, all without fanfare.

When the winds of progress blew away this agrarian society and the Industrial Revolution arose, the learning lifestyle grew increasingly rare. When parents had to leave the home to go to work, children left home to attend school. The "command center" of children's education shifted from the family home to the school.

The modern homeschooling movement is returning education to the home and community. Today's homeschooling families are reinventing a lifestyle from the past and making it appropriate for contemporary times. This means that most homeschooling families have accepted complete responsibility for their children's academic progress. When they take responsibility, something amazing happens. After a period of time (measured in months for some, years for others) and without conscious recognition that it's occurring, the families find themselves living what they often term "the learning lifestyle." Merely by accepting responsibility for academics, they become focused on finding or creating opportunities that involve learning—day and night, winter and summer, in work and play, formally and informally, at home, and everywhere else.

This, I believe, is why so many homeschooling families ultimately break away from school-schedule-type thinking. They can't help but witness their children learning in the morning during a visit to grandma's, in the afternoon on a walk with a naturalist, and in the evenings through dinnertime discussions. Their own *experience* provides enough proof that learning can happen any time, anywhere. (As with anything else, it takes more proof for some than others, so the length of time varies.) Then they make a transition from "doing school at home" to creating and living a "customized" learning lifestyle based on the beliefs and values most important to them. The learning lifestyle is the underpinning for homeschoolers' astounding success.

Anyone Can Live Like a Homeschooler

Ready for another big secret? Chances are great that you're reading this book to find out just what you need to do to or for your child to improve her school performance. In reality, much of what is necessary for your child's betterment depends more on changes for you, the parent, and how you create the lifestyle to support improved academic performance. Surprised? Many homeschooling parents are, too.

As a newcomer to the game of golf, I'm noticing in my environment all things golf. One comment about the game that I find particularly striking is that it isn't played on the vast acreage of the golf course as much as in the five and one-quarter inches between my ears. It's also in the head where a learning lifestyle begins, followed quickly by the heart. (At this point I can't help but hear the Field of Dreams' voice whispering, "Build it and they will come.") Build a learning lifestyle, and your family will live it. The following three actions follow the habit of trust outlined in the previous chapter to support your dream of helping your child excel.

1. OBSERVE

How does the gardener determine the best way to help her plants grow? Because she is interested in growing the finest plants possible, she grabs every opportunity to learn as much about them as she can. This may include a great deal of research and talking with experienced gardeners with knowledge of these same plants. It also involves lots of observation.

The gardener watches for clues about each plant's preferences—this one likes more sun; that one, a little more humidity. She observes each plant's nature—one seems to be putting more energy into roots while another develops a thick stem. She pays attention to what she does that helps that action, as well as to what fails so she doesn't make the same mistake again.

In a nutshell, this habit of observation is how many homeschooling parents learn how to help their children make the most of their learning time. In part two, Focus on Your Unique Learner, we'll go into more detail about the amazing array of learning styles and the clues that help you figure out your child's preferences. In the meantime, begin observing your child at work and play. To get you started on this interesting exercise, here are a few things to watch for.

- Give your child directions to accomplish a few new tasks. Which works better—telling her or showing her how?

- When your child independently starts to do a project, does he seem drawn to first read about it, hear about it, just start doing it and figuring it out as he goes along, or a combination of all of these methods?

- Watch your child settle down to homework. Does he choose a quiet area, or does he turn on a radio or gravitate to where activity is ongoing?

- When it's available, does your child seek out quiet time alone, or does she prefer to be around others?

- What does your child do with spare time? Build? Create? Read? Talk? Run? Think?

- What are his strengths? Weaknesses? How much does his best effort accomplish?

You'll think of many other situations to observe, and you may discover information you weren't even looking for. Ultimately, putting knowledge of your child's traits and preferences to work will contribute more to his academic success than just about anything else you can do for him.

2. GUIDE

Supported by your trust in yourself and your child and your growing storehouse of knowledge about your child's preferred means of learning, you will find this next homeschooling secret easy to understand. You don't need to be a trained, certified teacher to help your child learn! All you need to do is to begin thinking of yourself as a "learning guide."

The history of New York's Adirondack Mountains is replete with stories of men who made their living as guides for city folks looking for outdoor adventure. Visitors knew they could not survive in the vast mountain wilderness, so they hired the guides to make sure they didn't get lost, attacked by bears, or freeze or starve to death. The visitors were in charge and did all the work. The guides merely provided the direction necessary to keep everyone out of harm's way. If his charges were canoeing toward a waterfall, the guide warned of the danger and suggested a safer course. If it grew cold, guide and guests sat by the campfire discussing the best places to pitch their tents and how to dress warmly.

No one looked at the guide's job as that of teacher in the way public schools have trained us to think of teachers, as those who impart everything they know. Rather, he was hired to protect, advise, and, for the sake of his livelihood, ensure the experience was as rewarding and enjoyable as possible in the hope the tourists would one day come back for more.

In a similar light, many homeschoolers see themselves as learning guides. The children, as the learners, do the work. Mom and dad provide necessary resources, be they books, classes, or other people, then observe, consult, answer questions or explain when needed, and generally keep the child on a safe and productive course. They do their best to ensure that the experience is as rewarding and enjoyable as possible in the hope the child will eagerly come back for more.

3. ENCOURAGE

Two-four-six-eight, who do we appreciate? Johnny, Johnny, way to go, Johnny!

Most homeschooling parents I know are their children's most vocal cheerleaders. In a world where children often find themselves and their scholastic efforts unappreciated (wouldn't you feel your efforts unappreciated if the boss kept sending back your reports covered with red marks noting all your mistakes?), a successful homeschooled child's learning experience includes a large dose of encouragement.

You may encourage your child's learning experience in many ways beyond patting her on the back for a job well done (or, equally important, for a job well attempted to the best of her ability). Let your child hear you speaking positively of her accomplishments to others. Discuss your own learning challenges and successes at the dinner table so she gets the subtle message that learning is important to you and will be important to her throughout her life. Offer to proofread writing. Double-check math calculations. Talk about what you once learned from a good movie on her subject of study. Share a funny story from your own experience with the topic. Discuss her hopes for the future and talk about what she needs to know to create the future she desires. Find as many opportunities as possible for one-on-one conversations where you share positive expressions—most children want to live up to the expectations of those they love.

From One Parent to Another

STRONG FAMILIES

Families with children in traditional schools can enjoy many benefits of the homeschooling life. Why? Because living and learning with kids is amazingly natural for most of us, almost instinctive. After all, isn't this exactly how our ancestors lived, parents guiding children, learning together as families and using whatever methods and approaches were at hand?

The learning approach to family life strengthens the family in its natural—and rightful—role as a stalwart and respected institution in the community. The requirements are few, and most of what you'll do is a natural part of the normal parenting package, if parents only believe it. Parents who love to learn, who enjoy spending time with their children, and, most of all, who themselves brighten when the aha! light comes on in their children's eyes—these are the parents who find the learning approach to family life most satisfying and successful. As a stay-at-home parent, I found my life enormously satisfying because of our learning lifestyle, no matter what educational option we were using at the moment.

Launching a learning approach to family life in today's hectic world can begin with a simple change of priorities. You will learn to put the needs of family and family members first. Next, encourage everyone to get to know each other and their interests. Explore and learn together. You as parents will learn to slow down and listen to your children. Your children will know exactly who to turn to: mom and dad.

My advice is to start today. Talk with your family. Share music. Play games. Explore. Question. Follow your heart's desire and share it with your children, thereby showing them how to follow theirs. As you help your children discover their hearts' desires, you stand to learn more from them than they will ever learn from you.

Ann Lahrson Fisher, Carson, Washington

Ways to Create a Learning Lifestyle

Now that you're beginning to think like a homeschooling parent, let's look at ten ways you can set up the same kind of learning lifestyle for your regularly schooled child.

THINK MERGE, NOT JUGGLE

You've heard it before: "I'm juggling work and family." "I have to juggle housework and time with my kids and spouse." "I'm juggling college, work, and caring for my aging parents."

Much of the literature on raising children and/or creating a better life prescribes techniques to accomplish this juggling. Often, this is a prescription for disaster because even the most accomplished juggler sometimes drops the ball. When the ball is an important aspect of our lives, one slip can be devastating.

Much better to think in terms of merging life's responsibilities and blurring the lines between them as much as possible. Nowhere is this more crucial in a learning lifestyle than with your child's education, for to set up false boundaries between life and learning is to shortchange her, robbing her of the natural connections that enrich her existence.

Involve your child in your own career as much as possible. Bring home stories about your day, the different people with whom you work, and news of your own learning experiences. If applicable, tote some work home so your child can see what you do all day. (As a child, I honed my reading skills on the depositions my attorney father carried home in his briefcase.) Take your child to your workplace where she can soak in the sights, sounds, and smells of your environment.

Don't stop there. Think of all that is involved in running a household and find ways to move beyond the typical chores children do. Merge learning and living by working together to:

- Take inventory of food and supplies, make shopping lists, and shop

- Pay bills, then balance the checkbook

- Cook and bake (especially effective when your child is required to bring a dozen cupcakes to school or contribute to an organization's bake sale)

- Perform household repairs, upkeep, remodeling

- Garden, landscape, maintain the yard

- Maintain automobiles

By merging instead of juggling the activities you have to do anyway, you'll find yourself spending a lot more time with your child. Be forewarned that, initially, some of these activities will take a little longer as your child builds skill and knowledge, but if it's fun and interesting, her learning curve will be sharp, and you'll find you create more time in the long run for nonwork-related togetherness.

MAINTAIN (OR REDEVELOP) A SENSE OF WONDER

Living a learning lifestyle requires a desire to learn, and as a parent you have an incredible opportunity to become a resident role model. The lucky among us will have maintained the sense of wonder necessary to fuel this desire, and the rest of us simply need to redevelop it.

Samantha Bouyea brought two middle-school-aged sons home from a suburban Illinois school. No matter what she tried, she explains, the boys just weren't catching the "learning fever" she had read so much about in homeschooling books and magazines.

"Then, while working on a quilt for a charity fundraiser, I realized how much I missed the sewing and creating I used to do,"

Samantha says. "So I started up again. I got tons of material and started at least a dozen projects, including décor changes for my boys' rooms so they would be involved in decisions and maybe catch my enthusiasm. I devoured books and magazines and wondered out loud about new techniques."

In retrospect, Samantha realizes it was about this time her sons began asking to accompany her on her many trips to the library to pick up their own information about model trains, soccer, and astronomy, among other topics. They caught the learning fever through exposure to someone who had it!

PLAY

Play comes naturally to children, especially younger ones, for a reason. It is their life laboratory, a place where it's safe to experiment and connect unrelated pieces in myriad ways and to repeat skills (otherwise known as practice) until they achieve mastery. Play is curiosity and imagination's kingdom of infinite possibility. Play is at once a way for children to express—and get to know—themselves.

"I had to let go of the belief that play was a waste of time, nothing important, something kids 'should' do only when they finish what they are supposed to be doing!" remembers former teacher Sandra Strauss. "I now watch my children closely in their play. I am amazed at what goes on.

"My fifteen-year-old plays with his younger siblings," Sandra continues. "They share parts of themselves that often are considered silly. They let loose, they create, they mimic, they joke, they grow. Play is a child's 'work.' One thing I know I will be proud to say," she concludes, "is that my children lived a full childhood."

Expand the life laboratory of play and watch the positive effects on your learning lifestyle! Don't forget to join your children in play, too. Have a family powwow and discuss what kinds of play everyone is interested in doing. Think beyond board games and sports to find something everyone might enjoy. Sing, dance, exercise, paint, sculpt, hike, swim, fly a kite, build an igloo out of sugar cubes, solve a mystery, sew a quilt, perform magic tricks, create a stand-up comedy routine, take up photography.

The game you play is not as important as the fact that you make the time to play. Let down your hair and be open to the idea of learning on an equal footing with your child. Turn off the TV and telephone, relax, forget about the bills, and give over all of your attention. Playing together is the quickest way to get a learning lifestyle off to a happy start. Oh, and don't be surprised if you reduce your stress level at the same time.

REPLACE PASSIVE LEISURE WITH ACTIVE LEISURE

Professor Mihaly Csikszentmihalyi (no, I can't help you pronounce it!) has spent thirty years working to answer this question, among others: What makes a life useful and worth living? This prolific writer reveals the results of his research in several books about what he calls "flow." The professor, in *Finding Flow: The Psychology of Engagement with Everyday Life,* says flow is the metaphor "that many people have used to describe the sense of effortless action they feel in moments that stand out as the best in their lives."

Since the purpose of any child's education should include a good dose of creating a life that is useful and worth living, you may want to examine the professor's findings to see how they can contribute to your child's academic success. To this end we'll explore his ideas further in chapter 9. For now, we'll just touch upon Professor C.'s findings on flow as they relate to leisure activities.

Consider this scenario, repeated in millions of houses across America. After tired family members return home from work and school, prepare or pick up and then eat dinner, a little "mindless" activity, usually in the form of television viewing, rests the brain and nervous system. We often call it "unwinding."

But, Professor C. says, "Very rarely do people report flow (or those best moments of our lives) in passive leisure activities, such as watching television or relaxing."

The negative aspects of an abundance of television viewing have been argued since the square box arrived in homes en masse, but Professor C. makes a direct connection between too much TV (or other passive leisure) and a lack of quality of life. If this is true, the saddest part is that flow-producing active leisure "usually takes up only between a fourth and a fifth of a person's free time, and for many it is vastly overshadowed by the amount of time spent in passive leisure activities such as watching television."

Instead, the professor explains, we should do our best to create moments of flow that involve mental focus and effort (the reason some folks experience flow more often while driving than in any other part of their lives). How do we accomplish this?

"When people do a hobby, get involved in exercise, play a musical instrument, or go out to a movie or restaurant," Professor C. says, "they tend to be more often in flow than in any other part of the day."

The learning lifestyle seems to occur best when you "kill your TV" and get involved in activities that challenge and inspire, such as those you might choose to "play" with your family.

REGULARLY QUESTION ASSUMPTIONS ABOUT LEARNING

While play and active leisure are the physical aspects of a learning lifestyle, questioning assumptions about learning is the mental activity. If you've already begun to work on your definition of education, you're likely noticing how big an impact school and school attendance have on your life. "It organizes your day, your week, your year, your life," Elizabeth McCullough, a homeschooling mom of two who volunteers for the Virginia Home Education Association, points out. "The school my children attended issued a continuous stream of directives. I began to feel as if we weren't in control of our family life anymore."

So what's a good parent to do? "Say no every once in a while," suggests Elizabeth. "This helps you see it's in your power to decide the level of involvement you're comfortable with. Don't let anyone guilt-trip you if you think you're doing what's right for your child."

Speaking of guilt trips, if your child happens to be experiencing academic or social difficulties in school, you have a perfect starting place to question assumptions. Is the problem a learning disorder, or a teaching disorder? Is it lack of attention, or a boring curriculum? Is it hyperactivity, or a young child behaving like a young child? Is he really too shy, or is he just one of those quiet, introspective people?

The learning lifestyle involves a lot of thought, not just about the act and purpose of learning, but also about the who, where, when, why, and how it takes place, and what you as the parent can do to ensure your child gets the maximum benefit out of the time invested.

"Don't be afraid," Elizabeth advises. "Or rather, be afraid and do things anyway. You don't have to take your kids out of school. Just try questioning all those institutions and assumptions that you've been taking for granted and see what happens. Try going against the flow a little, and enjoy the freedom it creates."

LEARN SOMETHING

Want to know the secret of getting the hang of the learning lifestyle as quickly as possible? Learn something!

That's right, become your own guinea pig. Pick something you've always been interested in (interest is a key factor) but never took the time to study or try. I'm not talking about spending eight years becoming a doctor, just choose something you can teach yourself, maybe with the help of continuing education classes or an afternoon here and there spent with a friend, neighbor, or relative who knows a lot about the subject.

I mentioned earlier that I'm a newcomer to the game of golf, so I recently had the opportunity to take my own advice and watch how this old dog learned a new trick. As soon as I got my clubs, I asked my son to show me the basics, not in my living room, not through the pages of a book, but at a driving range where I could actually use the tools of the trade. I jumped in feet first, made every mistake conceivable, then went back to the range at every opportunity to try different ways to correct my mistakes. After checking out several books on golf from the library, I learned half a dozen drills and figured out what at least some of the lingo meant, at the same time visiting those vast expanses called golf courses with the goal of hitting the ball as long and straight as possible.

I managed to attend most of a golf clinic where one-on-one lessons worked wonders on my swing. On rainy Sunday afternoons I watched the pros, both male and female, on television. I picked up golf magazines at every airport and checked out Web sites when time allowed. I peppered every golfer I knew with questions, and many kindly agreed to put up with me on courses where ever more advice was never in short supply. Equally important, through it all I had a wonderful time.

This may sound familiar to many of you who were introduced to computers as adults long after your school years were over. What did you do? You learned to use them. You pushed a button here, asked a question there, read a bit, figured out what went wrong, and then practiced some more. The bottom line is: You learned.

Another important secret homeschoolers have discovered is that children are capable of quickly learning—and enjoying—in exactly the same way adults are. Once you've taken a good look at what creates an enjoyable and successful learning encounter for you, you can translate that into similar experiences for and with your child.

DISTINGUISH BETWEEN GREAT AND NOT-SO-GREAT EXPECTATIONS

In a September 2002 article in *Reader's Digest* called "Secrets of A+ Parents," writer Nancy Kalish noted a recent study by the University of Illinois that found "when dads or other father figures showed involvement and concern simply by asking their children about what they were learning, those kids did better in school." Children, we have long known, tend to rise to the expectations of the significant adults in their lives.

Expecting a child to do his best is a great expectation; expecting perpetual A's in a subject in which he has never shown an interest or talent is not-so-great. To expect your daughter to follow her dreams is great; to expect her to follow your dreams is not.

Great expectations are those that set a bar a child believes he can reach while honoring him as a unique individual. In fact, one of the three main conditions for Professor Csikszentmihalyi's flow experience is that "a person's skills are fully involved in overcoming a challenge that is just about manageable." In other words, the activity is not so easy as to be boring or so difficult as to cause anxiety. Walking the tightrope between great and not-so-great expectations requires the sensitivity that accompanies knowledge of your child's strengths as well as his weaknesses.

Sensitivity and knowledge will help you respect your child's individuality and at the same time go a long way towards keeping your expectations challenging and reasonable. Homeschooling parents have discovered that the learning lifestyle tends to create such necessary respect. With a clear view of who your child truly is, you will see the futility of—and potential harm from—comparing that child to siblings or to others the same age. Great expectations focus on the individual child's progress, while not-so-great expectations are those that take attention away from this essential focal point.

THINK OF YOUR ENVIRONMENT AS A LEARNING LABORATORY

If a man's home can be his castle then it can be his family's learning laboratory, too. Funny, isn't it, how we rarely think of our home this way? Yet as "command central" of your family life it's the perfect setting for children to become successful and achieve independence. In their home lab, children can manage and perform all those little chores that are important parts of our lives: Do the laundry, sew buttons and hems, balance statements for checking and savings accounts, monitor investments, pay bills, clean house, prepare and clean up meals, change the car oil and a flat tire, give childcare and eldercare, chop and stack wood, iron, fix a leaky faucet, plan a vacation, garden, mow the lawn, create a grocery list and shop (on a budget). To really learn about life, a little knowledge of psychology never hurts. And to prepare her for a challenge that will likely only grow more commonplace as your child grows, allow her to deal with computer tech support.

You're right—these aren't going to directly help in sophomore English, American history, or calculus class. Rather, proficiency in these tasks will help your child travel toward independence with an increased sense of awareness, responsibility, and likely, a tad bit more respect for what Mom and Dad do for them. This indirectly translates into academic success—when awareness, responsibility, and respect permeate one aspect of life, they cross over to other aspects, including school performance.

Notice that your learning laboratory is already well stocked so you don't need to run out and buy special "educational" materials. All that you need for your child to master everything on the list above is available in and around your home. To learn about life you use the stuff of life. Regular household items are your

TEN STEPS TO CREATING A LEARNING LIFESTYLE

Think merge, not juggle

Maintain (or redevelop) a sense of wonder

Play

Replace passive leisure with active leisure

Regularly question assumptions about learning

Learn something

Distinguish between great and not-so-great expectations

Think of your environment as a learning laboratory

Extend and enrich your child's school lessons

Get flexible

materials. When you live in the laboratory you can't help but inch forward into a learning lifestyle.

EXTEND AND ENRICH YOUR CHILD'S SCHOOL LESSONS

You want to always be aware of what your child is currently studying in school so that you can extend and enrich those lessons with family-centered activities that originate in your personal learning laboratory.

Former Secretary of Education William J. Bennett spends school nights on eighth-grade math with his son, Joseph, according to a September 2002 *Reader's Digest* article about homeschooling by Nancy Kalish. "We go over all the trouble spots and learn the new stuff together," says Bennett. "We're guaranteed to talk for thirty or forty minutes each day, which might not happen otherwise. In some ways, teaching my son is the hardest part of my day. But it's also the best part, because we're doing it together."

As homeschooling families have discovered, just because an activity begins at home doesn't mean that's the only place it can occur. Guide your child towards the information she needs to keep learning about a subject she finds interesting, even if her class has moved on to another topic. Visit museums, check out every book the library has on the subject, run a search together on the Internet, and let her keep creating related arts and crafts if she desires. Start thinking of the world as your child's classroom (we'll explore this idea in more detail in chapter 10), and you'll be amazed at the number of opportunities for exploration.

GET FLEXIBLE

You have planned a quiet evening—then you hear there's a meteor shower tonight. You were going to visit your mother this weekend—then a friend tells you the symphony is coming to town. You were on a quick trip to the supermarket—then your child spies a butterfly emerging from a cocoon on the side of the tree in the front yard.

Here is the secret to enjoying the learning lifestyle: Become and remain as open and flexible as you possibly can. Educational opportunities often arrive at the darndest times. If you're going to take advantage of as many as possible, you need to be able to let go of, or delay, planned activities to enjoy them. Sure, it's not always possible to postpone or subvert your agenda, but other quiet evenings are around the corner, you can visit mom next weekend, and the supermarket will still be open after the butterfly flits away. Granted, dinner may be a little late, but I guarantee no one will starve to death in the meantime.

Oftentimes, these spontaneous learning opportunities are the most informative for children and the ones they remember best. They're the ones that create the memories that bind your family together through the years, the ones you revisit during Thanksgiving dinner ten years down the line. Just as physical flexibility offers many health benefits, learning flexibility offers incredible intellectual benefits for your child's educational enrichment and success. There's one big difference, though, at least in my book. This type of "exercise" is a lot more fun.

CHAPTER 3

Believe in the Power of Your Love

L OVE CONQUERS ALL. A romantic thought, yes, but it's also descriptive of the power of the love only you, as a parent, have for that person who is your child.

At this point in your reading you may be thinking, "But I couldn't possibly become my child's learning guide! I'm too _____." (Fill in the blank with your choice of reasons: dumb, busy, impatient, poor, or just plain ol' afraid.)

Here's another secret to chew on. Many folks who heard of the idea of "life as their child's learning guide" and gave it a go, at first filled in the blank with self-derogatory words, too.

Some take a leap of faith, fly into the role anyway, and learn to believe in the power of their love. It's a lesson, they say, that can change the way they help their children with educational matters. They discover parental love connects them to the intelligence, time, patience, riches, and courage they need to be effective. Now we just need to take a look at how they do it.

Put Experts in Their Place

Our society's reliance on experts is helping to make many professionals rich, but at what price to all of us? Oftentimes, relying on experts involves giving over to someone else the responsibility for an action we should take ourselves. Each time we give away responsibility we slowly but surely, and often subconsciously, erode our self-confidence to some degree. Responsibility "muscles," left unexercised, atrophy just as do physical muscles. In the responsibility department we get weak, sloppy, and increasingly inclined to rely on the experts, because given the shape we're in, we need all the help we can get.

Home educator Elizabeth McCullough of Middleburg, Virginia, feels many parents turn over their power to experts long before their children are born and have let it become a habit by the time their children hit the front door of school. She remembers the results. "I felt tyrannized by educational experts. I was so filled with self-doubt that my parenting became tentative, unsure, and eventually, detached and ineffective," she says. "Even as I wondered why my children had so many problems I found myself turning to new experts to solve them. It was an endless cycle. Experts," she believes, "will run your life if you let them."

Elizabeth agrees no parent knows it all, but at the same time she realizes no one knows her child as well as she does—"or at least, they shouldn't," she explains. "Your child wants your listening ear, your caring support, your strength and wisdom, not some expert's."

She found her power by placing the experts into supporting, instead of starring, roles. Elizabeth chose to "listen to her 'gut'" and simply talk with other parents who were actually raising children, and not writing books about it. "Consider whether what an expert is calling a 'problem' might actually be within the normal range of your child's development," Elizabeth cautions.

She could be questioning what prompted doctors in the year 2000 alone to write nearly twenty million prescriptions for Ritalin, Adderall, and other stimulants used to treat Attention Deficit Hyperactivity Disorder (ADHD). (Reported in *USA Today*, July 17, 2001, "Connecticut Law Seeks to Limit Ritalin Use.") Prescriptions fly into drug stores 35 percent more frequently than they did in 1996, and in some schools, "as many as 6 percent of all students take Ritalin or other psychiatric drugs, according to the federal Drug Enforcement Administration." Interesting, isn't it, that the disorder was all but nonexistent just one generation ago?

Or maybe Elizabeth is talking about the plethora of labels experts put on children these days: ADD, LD, EH, chemically imbalanced, gifted, talented, honor student, behavior problem, and so on. These have become the experts' "parent trap."

"I bought into the labels because they convey the impression that what was previously baffling and frustrating is now transparent and manageable," she says. "All that's left to do is search for the cure, which has a way of remaining elusive indefinitely. Labels can be convenient and reassuring, but they don't change anything in and of themselves."

Once you have put the experts in their place and exercised your responsibility muscles, you will experience the power of your love growing stronger, along with your self-confidence. From self-confidence you will move to self-trust.

"Don't ignore red flags in your child's health, learning, or behavior, and seek help appropriately," Elizabeth concludes, "but be skeptical of fads."

Give yourself a chance to observe your child, tend to his needs, and search out helpful resources. As the person in the world who knows him best and loves him most, you can do what the expert can't do—accept, guide, and support him daily.

Trust Your Parental (Mother's and Father's) Instinct

Birds fly. Fish swim. Caterpillars make cocoons. Not one of them is "taught" to do so in the manner we usually think about being taught. Instead, it's all part of instinct or, as my dictionary defines it, "The innate aspect of behavior that is unlearned, complex, and normally adaptive."

We readily accept that instinct serves every other species well, so why do we give it short shrift when it comes to humans? Surely we're not the only species on earth lacking this valuable gift.

No. We are blessed with just as much instinct as any bird, fish, or caterpillar. The difference is we also can do an awful lot of thinking. We can "reason" our way out of acting on that "feeling," especially when action might disrupt the status quo. Unfortunately, we parents have had a lot of years of schooling that emphasized training our intellects, to the detriment of our innate intelligence.

Parents can counteract this by getting back in touch with their parental instinct and learning to pay it the attention it deserves. In Nashville, Kay Brooks, a state liaison for the National Home Education Network, boils it down nicely. "If it doesn't seem right—or seems right—start from there."

So practice. The next time you get a "feeling" about anything related to your child's education, don't immediately start thinking it away. Don't immediately assume your family life circumstances rule out options. Set aside preconceived notions, including any educational labels your child may have been given. Assume your feeling is valid, for this is the only way to discover if there's anything to it. Trusting your parental instinct will help you become more sensitive to your child's educational needs, improve your ability to guide her, and help her succeed.

Utilize Your Other Untapped Abilities

When was the last time you made a list of all the things you do well? If you haven't done so since grade school, or have never done it at all, get out a pen and piece of paper. Include all of your skills, not just academically related ones. Be specific: Instead of

IT'S ALL INSIDE

A mom single-handedly lifts a car off her child before it crushes him. A refugee with no food or water carries her sick child for days to reach medical care. We've all read and marveled at stories of parents who find superhuman strength when their children's lives hang in the balance.

That strength, born of love, is ever present in each of us. We don't need a calamity to uncover it. All we need do as parents is trust that the best way to help our children achieve life happiness and academic success is to take responsibility for leading them to it, the same way the parents in extraordinary circumstances take total responsibility for leading their children to safety. They take action in love, and whatever skills they need to accomplish their heroic tasks become available to them at the right moment. Parents who practice a learning lifestyle know there is an equal amount of power in their parental love when they apply it to their children's academic achievement.

Linda Dobson

---

writing "I'm good at math," write "I'm good at balancing the checkbook, maintaining the household budget, preparing an income tax return." If you make the potato salad that disappears at every potluck supper it graces, add, "I make a wicked potato salad" to your list.

If you've given your list some time and thought, you'll likely find it's a lot longer than you expected. (An interesting side trip with your list is to go through and note where you learned how to do these things. Lots of people are surprised to find that many of the things they do well, if not most, are the results of learning that occurred outside of school. Learning this lesson led me to start thinking about the "return on investment" of the years children are required by law to remain in school.)

You may also discover that the activities you're best at are the same ones you like doing the most and/or provide you with the most personal satisfaction.

Next, think about how you can share some of your expertise with your child in the context of a learning lifestyle. Let's take your killer potato salad as an example. Instead of preparing it all by yourself next time, invite your child to help. If you know your child would resist an outright assistant position, be a bit more covert about it. "I've got to get this potato salad made but I'm short on time. It would help a lot if you'll grab the celery out of the refrigerator and chop up three stalks."

Tell your child the story about how you got the recipe. Talk about how much people like it and wonder out loud what sets it apart from other salads. (There will be more on "thinking out loud" in chapter 12.) Once the celery is chopped, wonder out loud how many cups you have. Give your estimate and ask your child to also estimate. Chances are good he'll take it upon himself to measure just to see whose guess was most accurate. Ask, "Do you think that's enough or do we need more? Do you think we need just as much chopped green pepper—or less or more? "

With this sort of conversation you involve your child in the process. Involvement leads to interest. Being interested is the key here. An interested child receives the information willingly, and if it is offered in an informal manner, all the better. Instead of using worksheets, untold numbers of homeschooled kids painlessly learn and master fractions by making potato salad—or cookies or cakes or pizza. They pick up measurement of length by helping cut wood for the new doghouse or measuring cloth for curtains. By starting to help your child at a place where you feel competent (because you like doing it and/or receive the most personal satisfaction), you'll build the confidence necessary to venture into other, less familiar avenues.

Don't forget to also tap into your child's abilities. Children love the opportunity to share what they know. Could you live without ever knowing how to build a Lego robot? Sure, but why would you when homeschoolers have learned that turning the tables and becoming the student while their child becomes the teacher supports the learning lifestyle so effectively?

Even as you're getting comfortable swapping expertise within the walls of your home, begin thinking about the untapped abilities of everyone you know—friends, neighbors, relatives, and people in the community. Remember that the world at large is the ultimate classroom in which your child will learn about becoming an independent, confident, and successful adult. There will be lots more on enjoying this unlimited link to knowledge coming up in chapter 10.

Develop Trust in and Respect of Your Child

As a parent concerned enough about your child's life success to read this book, you've likely made sure your child's respect and trust in you is a cornerstone of your family life. But equally vital to tapping into the power of your love is your ability to reciprocate, to keep trust and respect flowing both ways.

Because ours is a culture that ordinarily provides little of either trust or respect to children, this can be a challenging place for parents to begin. It may sound corny, but the Golden Rule provides a good starting point: Do unto others (in this case your child) as you would have them do unto you. Homeschool author John Holt presents another intriguing approach: Treat children as if they are guests visiting from a foreign country. The guests are eager to learn all about your ways (in this case the adult world), but they need time to observe and participate in order to understand. We would never berate, ridicule, or lose patience with a foreign guest for being ignorant, yet we often act negatively toward children as they learn. Either of these starting points will go a long way in helping to get the trust and respect flowing.

"I started off homeschooling like the drill sergeant from your worst nightmare," remembers Carrie Sommers, three years into homeschooling three children in southern California. "I don't know what I thought might happen if we didn't hit the books at eight A.M. sharp, but I didn't want to find out. Around the second month or so, when everyone was thoroughly miserable, I found my middle child crying in bed one morning. I asked what was wrong, and she sobbed, "You don't care how I feel; you just care about getting everything done.""

Carrie is thankful for what she terms her wake-up call and the change it initiated in her relationship with her children. "How could I have thought getting the math done was more important than acknowledging and respecting my children's feelings? When I began considering *their* needs and desires alongside my own, the whole atmosphere improved," Carrie happily reports. "As a bonus, I discovered the world doesn't end if we don't have a book in our hands by eight A.M. sharp."

Creating a two-way relationship, instead of hierarchical or "equivalent" relationships, provides two key benefits to your family. First, it constantly replenishes those involved. Trust and respect are given out, they come back, they're given out, they come back. This is, after all, the way we build any truly sustainable relationship. Second, a two-way relationship opens our minds and hearts to the reality that we have as much to learn from our children as they do from us. We may lead them into the wonderful world of books, but they lead us into the wonderful world of their innocence. We may expose them to the order of mathematical systems, but they expose us to the order of human development. We may show them the rudiments of social behavior, but they can show us the rudiments of a healthier, happier lifestyle.

If you choose to travel them, trust and respect are two-way streets that can take your family a long way into many years enjoying a learning life together.

Know You've Got Everything It Takes

There's a notion floating around out there that there's something "different" about families who choose to homeschool. Jedediah Purdy, author of *For Common Things: Irony, Trust, and Commitment in America Today* (Knopf, 2000) and a young man who was homeschooled in West Virginia before heading off to Harvard and Yale, explains, "People seem to think there's some kind of trick or you have to be really amazing. Or," he adds, "they think their kids have to be amazing. None of that seems really right."

It *isn't* right. I think we often mix up homeschooling's pattern of cause and effect. We meet homeschooling parents who seem confident in their decision to homeschool. They seem to have a lot of facts to back them up. Their children seem happy and intelligent, maybe even a bit mature for their chronological ages.

Did these folks start off this way? Maybe *some* of them did, but I guarantee not all of them. Odds are better they began life as learning guides feeling uncertain, unprepared, and afraid to be proven incapable . . . and then what?

The misconception of which Jed speaks stems from people witnessing the *effect* of home education on family members, not what necessarily *caused* the home education. These seemingly "super" parents and children have spent some time believing in the power of their love by exercising responsibility muscles; accepting their instincts; discovering, honoring, and sharing their abilities; and trusting and respecting each other. This only makes them *look* amazing.

BELIEVE IN THE POWER OF YOUR LOVE

Put experts in their place

Trust your parental (mother's and father's) instinct

Utilize your other untapped abilities and seek out the abilities of others

Develop trust in and respect of your child

Know you've got everything it takes

So what's the secret here? There is no trick. These people are *us,* everyday adults and children. It's just that these parents have realized they already possess inside of them everything they need to succeed. They have chosen to believe in love, the love that only you, as parent, have for that person you call your child. And guess what? This "secret" works very well in a learning lifestyle that includes traditional schooling.

CHAPTER 4

Making Time

I N A CULTURE PERMEATED with two-income families, large homes, an emphasis on personal fulfillment, and a banquet of extracurricular activities for all, no one escapes the dreaded time crunch. And nowhere is this crunch felt harder than on those precious moments we spend together as family.

Along with wondering how well you'll do as your child's learning guide, you're probably wracking your brain to figure out where you'll find the necessary time to do everything. While many aspects of life play out unequally, we all have the same twenty-four hours in a day. It's how we fill them that matters. When your child's success in life is a top family priority, you'll want to spend as much time on it as possible.

Caveat

After spending the day in school, most children have had enough *school.* Try not to turn your child's every waking moment into some sort of lesson that you remember from your own days at school. Try to open up time to have fun together. Some of the most effective learning occurs when it's incidental to an enjoyable activity.

Time Is Your Secret Weapon

Rome wasn't built in a day, and it's unrealistic to believe that the learning lifestyle can be created so quickly, either. It's imperative to remember that your time is your child's most important educational resource. As any millionaire athlete will tell you, it takes focused attention to get really good at something. The more time you devote and the more attention you pay to a learning lifestyle, the better your family will become at it. There are no magic pills, packages, or software that can replace the essential educational resource of family time spent together.

At this point you understand that including your child in daily activities—from washing dishes to putting the snow tires on the car—can greatly increase the amount of time available for a learning lifestyle. But because your child spends a lot of time in school, you'll have to search for ways to increase the time you have at home for learning. Fortunately, there are lots of ways to do this, so you may pick and choose the suggestions that might work best for your family, or draw up your own plans, based on your family's unique life circumstances.

REAL MEALS

Does a "real" meal for your family mean turkey with all the trimmings, Chinese take-out, or hot dogs and beans? A real meal is all of the above because what makes it *real* isn't the food. It's the company, and the company's attention to each other.

I'm convinced that sharing meals as a family went out of fashion when extracurricular activities became more important than going home. Many of us remember the time when "extra" activi-

THE GUMBALL MACHINE

The brand new gumball machine sits empty atop the refrigerator. With half the family already out the door on the way to an appointment, the three-year-old eagerly eyes the machine. "I want gum, please."

"Here," says Mom reaching into the box of gumballs on the counter. "You can take two."

Stomping his foot, the three-year-old shouts, "No, I want *that* gum," as he points to the machine.

Mom removes the lid and pours gumballs until the machine's globe glistens with a rainbow of colors. The child already holds a penny retrieved from the coin jar. He waits patiently.

In goes the penny. Out pops a gumball.

"I have one, and it's a green one, right, Mommy?" the child asks as he turns the door knob.

Mom smiles. "It is one. It is green." She closes the door behind her.

Linda Dobson, The Art of Education: Reclaiming Your Family, Community and Self *(Holt Associates, reprinted 1997)*

ties took place after school and finished up in time for kids to get home for dinner. Even sports practices ended in plenty of time.

It's a different world today. In an online newsletter I just received from Forest Hills Health Online, I saw this:

I just turned fifty, so maybe asking this survey question is a sign of my age. When growing up, I can remember the quickest way to get "grounded" was not to be home on time for dinner.

One of my sixteen-year-old triplets came home from school the other day after watching a movie showing a family from the 1950s sitting down at the table having dinner.

He said to me that evening, "Dad, we look like a family from the 50s!" He meant no disrespect, but was just making an observation since we always are sitting down as a family to have dinner. The next day following classroom discussion, he said more than 90 percent of students indicated their families rarely have dinner together. For them it was mostly eat on the run or in front of the TV.

In today's schools, enrichment offerings have mushroomed, and many parents believe that participation gives their children an academic edge. A child can be busy after school straight through until bedtime, garnering sports, leadership, academic, musical, and organizational help guaranteed to improve test scores or some other academically important aspect of the child's life.

If your child is this involved, now is a good time to consider the return on investment—not just on your financial investment, but also the home time you and your child put into such activities and take away from family time. Factor in travel to and from the activity, and if selling candy bars and wrapping paper are part of the package, don't forget to tally up time spent doing this, too.

Now consider how you and your child might fill these hours if you spent at least some of them together at home. Think about how you can use this time with your child to contribute to his health, happiness, and growth. Could you go for a walk or a run? Visit an aging relative or friend? Would you have more time to assist with necessary school assignments? To take in a play or interesting lecture? Watch a video related to a school subject and discuss it? Spend more real meals together?

It's difficult, I know, to begin thinking about dinnertime as "educational" time, especially if you don't go over assignments or discuss the latest test your child passed or failed. Nevertheless, this is the time to include your child in conversation about the "grown-up" aspects of your and your spouse's lives, discuss current events, play silly games that strengthen creative and critical thinking, dream about or plan future family events, or figure out how you're going to help your friend move next weekend. Real life served up during real meals.

Learning guides find that the return on time invested in this way beats the return on many so-called "educational" activities. Real meal investments will not directly or immediately improve your child's score on the math quiz, but they will provide an opportunity for the two-way flow of trust and respect. They offer connection to real world issues and events that your child may not hear about during the day. They provide the material your child needs to build a strong sense of responsibility and self-esteem that will eventually improve every aspect of her school career, not just one quiz score. These investments are not get-rich-quick schemes. They take longer to build a noticeable return, but they last a lifetime.

CAR TALK

The homeschooling mom of one son in Tulsa, Oklahoma, Marcy Worth, told a support group meeting, "The car salesman called and said he just took a trade-in that fit in my price range, but, he added apologetically, 'the car doesn't have a radio, cassette player, nothing.'

"I tore down to the dealership and took the car for a spin," Marcy told the group. "It was in good shape, fuel efficient, and, I double- and triple-checked, didn't have a radio. An hour later I left the salesman scratching his head when, as I drove away, I told him what a wonderful 'learning car' it would be for my son."

Assuming daily life will always include those short—and long—stretches together in the car, you can turn this time into academic gold. First step—if you have a radio, turn it off when you pick up your child. He may protest at first, but it won't take long for him to get used to the peace and quiet.

Now you can play games, much as you do around the dinner table. (See *Carschooling* by Diane Flynn Keith, Prima Publishing, 2002, for ideas.) Now you can check out of your library an array

PUTTING DINNERTIME TO WORK

While you're breaking bread, fill your time together with some of these educational activities, according to your child's abilities.

Food Trivia: Where did the (potatoes, cheese, salt, salad, butter, bread, drumstick, etc.) come from? A tree, root, animal, which animal, plant, other?

Estimate: How many Cheerios, beans, olives, etc. are in the bowl or jar? (Yes, you have to count them to see how close the guesses are!)

Use the Clues: One family member leaves the room while the others choose a famous person. This can be an historical character from the time period your child is studying in school or simply someone everyone at the table knows a lot about. (Abe Lincoln, Mickey Mouse, Tiger Woods, Laura Bush, Mary Poppins, use your imagination!)

The exiled family member returns, and he doesn't know who "it" is. He figures it out by the "leading" questions the rest of the family asks as they dine. "What do you like best about going to the theater? I've heard that you always count your change very carefully—why is that?" (Abe Lincoln.) "Don't you get tired of your girlfriend wearing that big bow in her hair? Where did you get such a funny laugh? Where do you buy your gloves?" (Mickey Mouse.)

The one being interviewed fakes the answers until he "gets it," and then he answers the questions, revealing that he knows who it is. For example, instead of asking, "Am I Abe Lincoln?" he would say, "Well, my parents always taught me to be honest, so whenever I get change at the store I count it very carefully, and I always return what isn't mine."

Basket Cases: During the week, family members fill a basket with various items: newspaper articles, fortune from a fortune cookie, school paper, joke, riddle, thinking puzzle, or others. At dinnertime someone takes one item out of the basket and you all discuss it. You can do the same thing using a "word of the day."

How's Yours?: One family member leaves the room while the others choose something that everyone has: stomach, hair, bank account, job, mother, skin, car, teacher, wardrobe, bedroom, pet. The family member returns to ask each person individually, "How's yours?"

Each person answers in turn, trying not to give it away. For "skin" the answers might be: burned, spotted, thinning, stretched, constantly renewing, showing some wear and tear, functional, etc. Answers for "bank account" might be: needs some help, nonexistent, status quo, neglected, growing by leaps and bounds, closely watched, etc.

Toothpick Manners: After the kids have received some basic instructions in table manners, it's time to play "Toothpick Manners."

Place ten toothpicks at each person's place. Before you play, tell everyone you're going to see how well everyone knows table manners. Explain that every time someone notices another person *not* using proper manners, she can ask that person for one of his toothpicks. He must give it up—cheerfully. When you're finished with your meal, the person with the most toothpicks is the winner.

Game creator's warning: Be sure to set the proper tone for this game or it can turn into a battle. Emphasize from the beginning that this is for fun and learning, that there should be no fighting or whining during the game, and that people must give up their toothpicks willingly when "caught." You could even establish a rule that if someone argues about what she was or wasn't doing, she has to give up two toothpicks. Also explain that you are only pointing out each other's mistakes as part of a learning activity. To do so in real life isn't proper and can be quite antisocial.

(continues)

PUTTING DINNERTIME TO WORK *(continued)*

Here is a list of basic table manners that may be used for this game, or be creative and make up your own.

- No elbows on the table

- Place your napkin in your lap

- Wipe your mouth with your napkin

- Chew food with mouth closed

- Say "please" when asking someone to pass an item and "thank you" when you receive it

- Don't talk with your mouth full

- Use utensils, not fingers, to eat (except for bread and other obvious finger foods)

- Don't belch, slurp, or make other uncouth noises during dinner

- Do not tip back your chair

- Place your utensils on your plate between bites, and lay them neatly on the plate at the end of the meal

- Ask to be excused before leaving the table when you have finished

Adapted from Jamie Miller's 10-Minute Life Lessons for Kids: 52 Fun and Simple Games and Activities to Teach Your Children Honesty, Trust, Love and Other Important Values *(HarperPerennial, 1998)*

of books on tape and enjoy and discuss the stories together. (This tactic has been known to change the minds and hearts of reluctant readers.) Now you can read maps, guess how far it is to your destination, and sing songs (yes, I *really* mean this). Now you can talk—about anything under the sun, including but hardly limited to, school.

LATE TO BED, EARLY TO RISE

Going to bed late or rising early as a method of stretching time needs little explanation. Lots of parents, particularly those who hold jobs, find they can extend their days on the front end or the back end, depending on their schedules. This method also works well for families in which one parent's work schedule keeps him or her away at the times the children are normally up and about.

Just like adults, children can be either early birds or night owls, so watch for these tendencies in your child and decide the time of day that works best for her. You don't want to turn your early bird into a late night grouch, or your night owl into a walking zombie at dawn. If you do this right, you just might find yourself sharing time with your child at her best, either before or after the stress of a hard day. You'll probably find these are often the best times to talk through challenges, be they homework, tests, or book reports left for eleventh-hour completion.

Children of all ages need lots of sleep, so don't create time by subtracting sleep. If your child will awaken earlier, adjust bedtime accordingly. With a school schedule to keep, it's a lot harder to allow your child to sleep later in the morning if you want to extend the back end of the day, so you may want to reserve this "time maker" for weekends if you've got a night owl on your hands.

MAKING THE MOST OF WEEKENDS

Ah, the weekend is here—you have two days to accomplish a month's worth of chores, and wouldn't it be nice if just once you could reserve one day for some much needed and well-deserved R & R?

It may sound funny, but those who live a learning lifestyle often don't differentiate between weekday and weekend. Any day, they reason, is a wonderful day to learn something new. So how do you combine the responsibilities of running a home with improving your child's academic outlook?

We're right back to inclusion again. Include your child in those tasks associated with living as a family. Cooperatively accomplishing chores provides many valuable "side effects." First, your child gets a chance to share and shoulder some responsibility for the family's welfare. In fact, the experience of assuming responsibility helps children become even more responsible. Second, by working together for and as a family you strengthen family ties and further build mutual trust and respect. Third, there's even more time for talk. Fourth, because many hands really do make light work, you'll get done faster and free up even more time for enjoyable activities that educate everyone.

If you are a parent whose weekends constitute most of your family time, this is your opportunity to take advantage of *quantity* time. Plan for your Saturdays and Sundays (and some Mondays if your job allows you to enjoy the federal holidays) all those activities that require larger amounts of time to accomplish or do well. When you're on top of what's happening in your child's academic life, you'll know well ahead when the science project or research paper is due. Weekends give you clusters of hours to help your child choose and plan her task in an attempt to make what she *has* to do as personally rewarding and stimulating as possible.

Do you remember research papers from school? I sure do. They began in elementary school and followed me year after year straight through high school. Pick a state. Pick a country. Pick an author. Pick a battle. Pick a political party. Pick a recipe. Prepare a paper/talk/demonstration/relief map on the topic.

Choosing a topic with only a child's perspective on the world is more like throwing a dart at a map than a well-thought-out decision. You can help your child make a sensible choice and in the process make the study more valuable. Let's take "pick a state" as an example.

- Ask your child if there's any state he's ever thought might be fun to visit someday. Why?

- Tell him about the states you've already visited or lived in and what you liked or didn't like about the food, people, landscape, traffic, or attractions.

- Talk about regional climates. Would he prefer to experience the dry heat of the southwest or the damp cold of the northeast? Would he rather see a cactus or a redwood?

- Touch on family history. Was great-great grandma born in a cabin in Tennessee? Did really great granddaddy land in Massachusetts aboard the *Mayflower*? Where did mom grow up? How does Uncle Joe like living in Nevada?

- Look at a map. Which states have mountain ranges? Border the ocean? Are big or small? Were original colonies? Were created during westward expansion?

- Think about your child's interests: Perhaps he doesn't know (or has temporarily forgotten) the Basketball Hall of Fame is in Springfield, Massachusetts; the factory that manufactures his favorite candy, Jelly Belly, is in Fairfield, California; Britney Spears was born in Kentwood, Louisiana. (Can't you just see a flood of research papers on Louisiana coming on?)

Now, instead of making an arbitrary choice, thanks to your attention and input your child can choose a state he's interested in and feels a connection to. His research will take on real meaning. It's easier for your child to remember Sacramento is the capital of California after he discovers it's that large city just forty miles away from the Jelly Belly factory.

Use the larger blocks of weekend time to help with these big decisions and projects. Additional time spent on the front end of the task, guiding your child toward meaningful learning, will save countless hours in the long run.

THINKING FUN

Be a Movie Title: Everyone comes to dinner dressed like a movie (or book or song) title. (Invite extended family or friends for even more fun.) Example: Wearing green pants with an arrow taped across the rear is *The Green Mile*.

Clues Around the House: Pick a title topic (movies, books, songs) then place objects around the house as clues for players to guess titles and write them down on a numbered sheet of paper. Really stretch your child's mind by having her prepare the clues! Examples:

Six pennies = *Sixth Sense*

Picture of the White House = *Casablanca*

Indian feather stuck in a heart-shaped photo frame = *Braveheart*

Compass next to an eaten apple = *East of Eden*

A written alphabet with the "D" missing = *Gandhi* (Gone D—okay, so it depends how you pronounce it)

A picture of Halle Berry = *Black Beauty*

The Name Game: This works best with six or more people sitting in a circle. Everyone has a partner and receives five (or more, depending on group size) slips of paper for writing a name. Names should be those that everyone in the group will know and may be of persons dead or alive, real or fictional, from history, current events, movie stars, singers, or sports figures, depending on the ages of those playing. Papers go into a bowl or basket.

One team of two starts. One partner opens one paper at a time and describes the person to the other partner as quickly as possible. "This is the president of the United States." "This is the man responsible for September 11." "This is the guy who played Forrest Gump," etc. The team has thirty seconds (or more for younger children) to guess as many names as possible. When the guess is correct that name is discarded.

Rules: If the "giver" doesn't know who the person on the paper is then he has to describe the name. If it's "Tiger Woods," the giver might say, "It's not a lion but a ____, and his last name is like a forest." You can't pass or put the paper back—you describe the best way you can.

If the partner hasn't guessed a name when the time is up, that name goes back into the bowl for someone else to pick it again.

Keep track of scores if you like and pass the bowl to the next couple.

The second time around the circle, the former "giver" becomes the "guesser" and vice versa. Play until all names in the bowl are gone.

LEARNING LIFESTYLE VACATIONS

Vacations represent the ultimate in blocks of time available to families. Why not turn your next one into a field trip extraordinaire?

One family I know spends their vacation attending a music camp together. Another reaches steadily toward its goal of visiting every Civil War–related historic site. Yet another packs up the kids and heads off on an annual quest to learn how to do something new. This year it's scuba diving.

Vacations offer a unique opportunity to families living the learning lifestyle. When you go away, you leave behind all those household chores, and hopefully all of the phone calls, overtime requests, and schoolwork, too. You can focus on learning with vigor.

Learning vacations don't need to be expensive to be interesting. They can start with car talk as you're on your way to the airport or driving to your destination. Something as inexpensive as a lakeside campsite can be home base for treks into the woods, swimming, snorkeling, and boating. Conversations with locals elicit information about the best fishing hole and the name of that beautiful flower. The gentleman camping in the site next to yours will be more than happy to tell you about the bears he encountered a few years ago while camping in upstate New York. Evening campfires offer a warm gathering place to review the day's events and make plans for tomorrow.

Notice that not once did I mention a school subject, yet this entire day is an extended learning experience. Biology, botany, geography, machines (if the boat has a motor), organizational and social skills, and phys ed—they're all in there. At first, you may think it's impossible that your child can learn very much while enjoying a vacation day. After all, the lessons are not as clearly delineated as when a specific lesson appears on a specific page in a textbook and everyone must focus on the same little piece. The secret is to focus your attention on all of the opportunities as you go about a learning lifestyle vacation, and lessons will unfold as a seamless whole with no need to label them.

You can apply these principles to any vacation anywhere. Keep the goal in mind, and choosing your next destination will be an interesting and fun proposition.

PLAY HOOKY

I know. I'm awful for even suggesting you take the old-fashioned hooky route, but many learning opportunities pop up totally out of sync with school schedules.

This is most definitely an area in which you need to be very careful in creating time. The increasing emphasis on achievement in schools makes playing hooky not as easy as it once was. Many schools have instituted inflexible absentee policies that allow only a certain number of missed days before there are serious repercussions. For example, in one Texas school, credit for the class is denied after ten absences, and in some New York schools, formal sanctions include referral to Child Protective Services or the Department of Probation.

Check your school's attendance policy (it may be online; my Google search on "school attendance policy" yielded 1,180,000 hits) and proceed with caution. Remember, your child could get sick or a family emergency could strike at some later time during the year, making it necessary to take time off. But, hey, if it's June and there are three absentee days available before the truant officer graces your doorstep, you *could* hit that astronomy club demonstration of telescopes that ends at midnight or go see that play you know your child will love even though it's a few hours' drive away, or...

SOLICITING OPT, OTHER PEOPLE'S TIME

When investors want to extend the power of their pocketbooks they turn to "other people's money." When you're looking to extend the power of learning time, why not turn to "other people's time"?

If they are available, grandparents are extremely valuable resources in the time department. For many children, time with grandma and grandpa is special indeed. Let the grandparents in on your new way of looking at life and invite their full participation. Most grandparents are delighted to be pulled into service.

"My three children are grown now, but many of their most memorable learning experiences involved my mom and dad," says Sylvia Mussaw of Houston, Texas. "When they were younger, Mom made fractions tasty by patiently baking cookies with them and brought new information into their lives by visiting every nearby museum," Sylvia remembers. "Before their visits, Dad would go to the library and bring home bagfuls of books he thought would interest them, and they held marathon reading sessions while snuggling on the couch."

As Sylvia's children—and the grandparents—got older, the children helped out with the elders' garden and home maintenance. "While the kids visited, Mom made sure to pull out an old photo album and talk about relatives deceased or far away, and Dad took them out to check for harmful insects in the garden, all the while passing on his vast knowledge about growing flowers and vegetables," says Sylvia.

Besides grandparents, solicit the aid of uncles, aunts, cousins, neighbors, and any and all friends. Extra special are people with knowledge and experience in areas that interest your child. When these folks understand what you are doing and why, most will be thrilled to become part of your team. If you run into that occasional stick-in-the-mud, don't take it personally, and move on. Generally, people love to share what they know, especially with a wide-eyed young person with some enthusiasm for the topic at hand. Regularly invite an interesting person to dinner with your family. You'll be amazed at what *everyone* at the table learns.

GIVE YOUR SCHEDULE A "SPRING CLEANING"

Spend a few weeks watching where your time goes. If you're the kind of person who can keep track of the hours with pencil and paper, so much the better. This exercise usually highlights at least a small portion of time you could put to better use. Consider also your extracurricular activities and gauge their relative importance to your goal of helping your child succeed in school and life. Many of us today are overextended to the point where we've forgotten that "charity begins at home." Because your child is only young once and ever so briefly, perhaps some of your commitments can wait until your child doesn't require as much of your time and attention.

Homeschooling parent Melissa Conrad began to question how much time she spent cruising her Elizabeth City, North Carolina neighborhood taking her four children to various activities.

When she calculated she was well on the way to putting 75,000 miles on her car that year, she knew something had to change.

"We sat down that night as a family with everyone's schedule, one copy of a map of our local area for every day of the week, and pencil and paper," says Melissa, "and went to work mapping our daily travels. Using this information, we created 'an ideal schedule' by grouping activities by geographic location and time. Then I called to change the day or time of every activity on our schedule that could possibly be changed, moving as close to that ideal schedule as possible. We mapped out the *new* schedules, a wonderfully educational experience in and of itself. Not only did we discover we'd cut the weekly mileage almost in half," Melissa reports, "the schedule now puts me near the grocery store at a time when I only have the two youngest children with me, allowing me to give them the same time and attention for 'grocery store math' and other learning experiences as the two older children received. I was amazed at how much time this exercise saved me."

If you're unable to find a few more minutes per day or hours per week on your own, scour your library's shelves for books on time management. Popular titles include *Time Management from the Inside Out: The Foolproof System for Taking Control of Your Schedule and Your Life* by Julie Morgenstern (Henry Holt, 2000) and *The Procrastinator's Handbook: Mastering the Art of Doing It Now* by Rita Emmett (Walker and Company, 2000).

As the authors of both these books explain, the point isn't to turn your home into an army boot camp, but rather to apply time-management principles to your unique life.

Keeping Quality in Your Newly Found Time

Now that you're figuring out ways to gather together enough minutes to spend on your child's academic life, remember to fill the new time with as much quality as possible. The point, you

EIGHT WAYS TO MAKE TIME FOR ACADEMIC EXCELLENCE

Eat real meals together

Turn off the radio so that you may talk or play fun learning games while in the car

Go to bed later or get up earlier

Make the most of your weekend time together

Turn vacations into the highlights of your learning lifestyle

Help your child play hooky as often as you legally can

Solicit other people's time to contribute to your endeavors

"Spring clean" and organize your time

recall, is to keep alive or, as is often necessary for older children, to rekindle the joy of learning that your child used to feel.

Harking back to my own days in school, I remember how often the teacher gave assignments or instructions and then left us to our own devices to complete the work as proof that we had "learned" the new concepts and information. I think of this as the "teacher say, children do" method of teaching. Many of us still think of this as "the way" learning happens. So pervasive is this thinking that we often continue the trend at home with our children. We give them a great educational toy, activity, book, or video, then send them off to enjoy it or figure it out alone.

Not the way to go, say homeschoolers who find that learning time is most fruitful when parent and child spend it together, interactively. "Engage children in active, not passive learning," writes

Becky Mollenkamp in an August 2002 article called "Learning from Homeschool Families" in *Better Homes and Gardens* magazine. "That means turning off the television and spending quality, interactive time together, not just in each other's presence."

A homeschooling father whom Becky interviewed, Paul Mech, summed it up well: "Time is the biggest gift a parent can give to a child. It tells the child, 'You are worth it to me, you are valuable to me, your happiness is my concern.'"

So What About *You?*

We've addressed everything time-wise except for one issue: finding the time you need to accomplish your own goals and pursue your own dreams. Parents shouldn't forget about their own needs, but they also need to be realistic and realize they can't have everything at the same time. "Many homeschooling families sequence their life's goals," explains Ann Lahrson Fisher, a Washington-based homeschooler since 1979 whose two daughters are fully grown. "It's family life and homeschooling now, and other personal goals are achieved before and after, with lots of compromise along the way. Many people are much happier with a 'sequencing' approach to their lifestyle. Some examples would be college, career, then children; or children, then college, then career, and the dozens of permutations that work in combination for different families."

Only you can decide the sequence that best serves your family's unique needs and circumstances. One thing's for certain: Only when you're happy with your time plan will you be able to give your child the joy and attention she needs to succeed. Make sure this part of your family's lifestyle is well thought out and flexible enough to accommodate unforeseen yet inevitable changes in family members' needs.

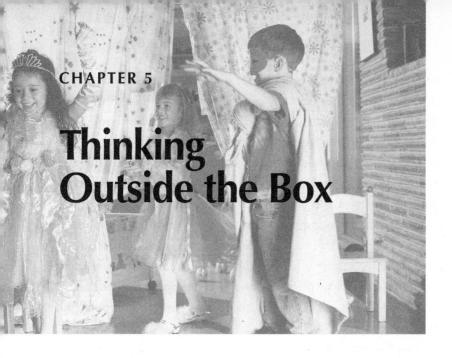

CHAPTER 5

Thinking Outside the Box

TODAY'S PARENTS face a lot of potential educational reforms we never heard of just ten short years ago. Who would have thought the idea of vouchers would fly? Or that a growing number of states would authorize charters allowing folks with a plan to try different approaches that might work better for some students? Or that schools would race to be next in line to provide their offerings in a computer-based format for students who stay home?

Imagine a scale from one to ten that gauges change in the way children are educated. Let's start with what most of us are familiar with, public and private schools, as number one on the scale. Here's where homeschoolers have uncovered an important secret: Vouchers, charter schools, and school curriculum delivered online sit somewhere around 1.00001 on our scale, a mere fraction of change away from existing schooling.

Looking at the system from the outside gives parents like you and me a very different perspective than the one other families get only from the inside. Families who live and learn outside the system have, to varying degrees, experienced great changes in many ways. They experiment with scheduling, use different books, and eschew standardized testing. They socialize with different age groups, allow their children to learn how to read before and after the age of eight, and play card games to learn multiplication. From this perspective, vouchers, charter schools, and an online school curriculum occupy the same box as traditional schooling.

To make effective use of the "tricks" homeschoolers know, you might try taking a leap of faith that lands you outside that box. Think about the possibilities of real change, a really different way of looking at education. Then plan to enjoy what you'll find outside the box.

The following list of starting points for thinking outside the box is, admittedly, subjective, and lists other homeschoolers put together would likely differ somewhat. Nevertheless, I hope you'll enjoy them and that they will inspire you to seek out even more.

You Don't Have to Go Along Just Because Everyone Else Does

Many of us cringe at the idea of going against the flow, making waves, blowing the whistle, rabble-rousing. I've lost count of the number of parents who say that one thing or another was wrong with their children's education, yet they chose not to do anything about it. Parents have many reasons for keeping quiet.

They may think, nobody else is complaining so maybe it's just me being ultra-sensitive or too picky or paranoid. They know the teacher or the spouse/child/best friend who is the source of the problem and don't want to get the person in trouble. They think, the school already has enough troubles. They fear an upheaval might take the child away from his friends. They fear repercussions for the child in the classroom. As black sheep, they fear PTA meetings sure won't be what they used to be.

When it comes to your child's education, it's okay to be ultra-sensitive, picky, and even a bit paranoid. If you're looking for academic success, you need to keep your child on the top of your priority list. "Make choices for *your family*," Kay Brooks reminds us. "Don't let the system make those choices for you."

Going along with everyone else often occurs because of *not* knowing the details of your child's school program. "Home-schoolers have intimate knowledge of what is being taught to their children," says Kay.

Knowledge is indeed power, so step outside the box and familiarize yourself with your child's studies. "Ask for copies of the textbooks to read and check online sources for reviews of those textbooks," Kay explains. "Ask the teacher—and your child—what is being covered and how. Ask why you may not be seeing homework or journals. Let the teacher know, in a nonadversarial way," says Kay, "that you are paying attention."

Your child will be astutely aware of your interest in her studies, a fact research shows improves a child's desire to do well in school. While standing up against the crowd is at first a scary proposition, once accomplished it provides the satisfaction of having done the best thing for your child and also makes it easier to do it again in the future, not only with regard to your child's education but in other aspects of life.

Children Are Complete Persons As-Is

In our culture, we generally treat children as less than whole. From outside the box this appears a rather egotistical attitude on the part of adults. We behave as if children need this, that, and a good dose of the other thing—from us, of course—before we can take them as seriously as we take our friends, coworkers, and other adult acquaintances.

"Think in terms of child/person," explains Lillian Jones, still living the learning lifestyle in Sebastopol, California, even as her homeschooled son is off to college and work. "A child is not in training to be a person but is one already." What a difference this change in viewpoint can make in the lives of our children!

First, it allows us to see who they really are, not who we are hoping to "make," or even "help," them become. It stops us dead in our tracks if we begin to act as the creator who can mold and sculpt until we make a product we like. Seeing children as complete allows us to respect who they are, and we know that children who live with respect learn respect. In this way we feed their subconscious with messages of acceptance and love that negate any messages they receive to the contrary. In this way they develop a sense of self-created responsibility for what they say and do, and this leads to the mature thought and action that will guide them safely to and through independence.

In addition, in explaining "flow" as we saw in chapter 2, Professor C. reminds us, "The findings of science may have hopeful things to say to each of us. In the first place, they make us increasingly aware of how unique each person is. Not only in the particular way the ingredients of the genetic code have been combined, yielding instructions for developing unprecedented physical and mental traits. But also unique in the time and the place in which this particular organism has been set to encounter life. Because an individual becomes a person only within a physical, social, and cultural context, when and where we happen to be born defines a single coordinate of existence that no one else shares." Your child is not only complete, but stunningly unique. Allow this view to permeate every interaction with your offspring, and watch the results.

It's a good idea to share this thinking outside the box with the other adults who populate your child's life. Communicate with your child's teacher(s), again in a nonadversarial manner. Use that time during parent-teacher conferences, schedule a meeting, write a letter, send an e-mail, or make a phone call (the first two options are best as they allow for face-to-face discussion). Explain you want her on your team of influential adults in your child's life who, in making his academic success a top priority, are viewing—and therefore treating—your child in a different manner. (Of course when she does so, she will also do it for your child's classmates and benefit everyone.) Feel free to utilize the analogy of a foreign visitor from chapter 3.

Do the same with other adults—grandparents, soccer coach, and the neighbor whose lawn your child mows. The maturity that people recognize in homeschooled children doesn't derive from special textbooks or accelerated classes. It grows from daily living with the same respect we parents give our fellow adults.

Mutual respect can transform a less-than-perfect relationship with your child. Once you accept her as already complete, you will find that the time and energy you used to spend trying to coax, help, or otherwise encourage her to become something different, you can now use in a more positive way, encouraging and supporting all that she already is.

Don't Divide Life into So Many Boxes!

One reason parents place so much trust in the education we see in traditional schools is because we have inherited the view that life can be divided into subjects, good and bad, or black and white. If we continue to hold onto this view, we find ourselves frustrated and confused, because those divisions don't hold true beyond the schoolhouse doors.

"Entering college was a shock for most of my friends and me," homeschooling dad Lester McCarthy recalls. "Education became, I don't know, 'bigger' in the sense that suddenly no one put limits on how you connected the dots, on what your mind could consider. The only thing I can compare it to is how I think newborn babies must feel when removed from the womb, then from swaddling. They're physically startled when they get out of their 'compartment' and feel their place 'in the whole' for the first time. It was mentally startling at first to live without intellectual compartments and to experience it all as a whole."

Lester and his wife, Cathy, chose homeschooling with the hope this won't happen to their two boys when they head away from their Rhode Island home toward college. "We want them to grow up knowing there aren't any compartments out there," says Cathy, "because it's never too early to connect the dots—that's what real learning is all about."

Here's a most interesting and valuable lesson homeschoolers have learned. When you think outside the box, you see there really isn't any box at all! It's much like the enlightening moment Dorothy and her friends experience in *The Wizard of Oz* when Toto pulls back the curtain and reveals "the powerful Oz" to be a mere mortal who can't really grant their hearts' desires at all.

In the story a wonderful transition occurs. Dorothy and her friends realize the power necessary to make the changes they want resides within them. They need only to believe, and they can accomplish their goals.

So how do families learn to believe in themselves enough to rediscover their own power, let go of life's illusionary boxes, and see learning weaving in and out of the "whole" that is life? "Parental learning guides reintegrate the world and find their places in it," explains Elizabeth McCullough. "For starters, make a list of everything you're not good at but always wanted to try. By the way, very young children do this naturally; they haven't yet learned that not being good at something is an acceptable reason to not try—they don't know that failure is bad. Have your child try this exercise with you, or at least share your list with your child."

You're not getting off *that* easy. There's more, says Elizabeth. "Pick something from your list and try it. It can be anything; maybe something peaceful and soothing like gardening or energetic like karate. Assume from the start that you will fail, perhaps several times. Cultivate the attitude that learning is a process, not an outcome (i.e., getting there is half—all—the journey). If the thought of trying something new scares you, great!"

Behave and think as if there are no boxes, and they will slowly disappear. Be your child's role model. Create for your child as much time for real-world observation, experience, and wide-ranging reading on topics that interest her, and, like Dorothy, she will realize, "There's no place like home."

Teaching Is Not Essential to Learning

"Children/people are natural born learners," explains Lillian Jones who, after studying as a student teacher, changed her mind about getting a teaching degree. "This shouldn't come as such a surprise to us, but it does, because so many of us experienced an educational method that taught us we learn only from being taught."

Like other parents, Lillian had to first think outside the box in order to discover the broader perspective for herself. For Lillian, as for countless other families, it took failed attempts to recreate school at home to show "teaching, more often than not, isn't a necessary ingredient in learning."

You can simply tell your child this, but he may not believe you, because his educational experience provides evidence to the contrary. Much better is to *show* him within the context of your life together. When your child understands he doesn't have to wait for someone to teach him something and that he may easily learn things he's interested in, education becomes something exciting, useful, and valuable. Sharing the experience strengthens family ties.

Figure out a new computer program, or exercise workout, or furniture assembly—together. Point out how you're both "learning on the fly." Conduct your thought processes out loud. Consult sources of information. Talk about other tasks you've taught yourself to do. Ask questions. Answer questions. Note how satisfying it feels to figure things out yourself. Celebrate victory, and learn from defeat.

There Are As Many Ways to Learn As There Are to Skin a Cat

We'll soon cover in-depth the many different learning styles humans possess, but for now we'll settle for enjoying thinking outside the box where differences are not just accepted but appreciated. Such appreciation begins at home. Here you can expose your child to many different ways of learning, so that when you happen upon one or several that "click," the educational box opens up and your child feels the sweet experience of achievement.

"Parents give their children a wide variety of food to keep them healthy," explains Ann Lahrson Fisher, author of *Fundamentals of Homeschooling: Notes on Successful Family Living* (www.nettlepatch.net/homeschool). "Like many other parents, the most successful homeschooling parents help their children find information in a variety of ways, too. Keeping many doorways to learning as wide open as possible really enhances a child's ability to learn."

With her two daughters Ann used the "Rule of Three" to make sure they were exposed to a variety of learning approaches. "I let the girls explore the topic in at least three very different ways," she says. "If one of them was struggling with a particular topic, such as history or science, I just mixed and matched until I found a method that fit."

Once you've opened the box and found all the possibilities, you'll also see that sometimes, the same child requires a different approach for a different subject. "For example," explains Ann, "I learn most things best through reading, listening, and mental processing. Love those philosophy lectures, but don't try to explain math to me! To learn a new math concept," Ann continues,

"I am at sea without models and drawings, and listening to talks or lectures puts me right to sleep. Go figure."

Learning Happens All the Time

We hear it constantly, first from educators and, more recently, from politicians who have latched on to education as a "hot button" issue: We need to get children ready to learn.

Some parents have discovered there's nothing one can do about children learning. Sound defeatist? Actually, the opposite is true. Learning is just something children do. All the time. Even when no one is teaching. Talk to these parents, and you're sure to hear stories of six-year-olds learning to read seemingly by osmosis and twelve-year-olds who never even glanced at a textbook who are ready for college math.

Look at Jacob Powell who spent his formative years in northeast Michigan as a very young businessman. He started with a paper route and moved up to door-to-door greeting card sales. Then, as a teen, he began a home-based mail-order business, learning what he needed to know as he went along. "I knew Jacob was continually learning about numbers even though we never followed any math curriculum. When he decided he wanted to go to college," says his mom, Lynn, "he picked up a couple of math texts from the local college bookstore, studied for a few months before taking the SAT, and scored well enough to head off to the college of his choice. It's amazing what kids can do when we give them a chance."

Lillian Jones' son was seven years old when he was very sick and home from school. "For days he looked like he was bored stiff lying in front of the television and a public television science program," she says, "but when he felt better he greeted his dad at the door and told him all about the wonders of atoms! I didn't think he was even watching or listening."

STARTING POINTS FOR THINKING OUTSIDE THE BOX

You don't have to go along just because everyone else does

Children are complete persons as-is

Stop dividing life into so many boxes!

There are as many ways to learn as there are to skin a cat

Teaching is not essential to learning

Learning happens all the time

From inside the box we think we need to get our children "ready" for the rigors of school. Thinking outside this box—starting with the premise that children are learning all the time—we see *what* they learn is the important element. This wonder guides the A+ parent to a place that best helps her child.

Accept that children learn all the time, and you'll pay more attention to what you say to and about your child, spouse, neighbor, deliveryman, child's teacher, and computer. You'll be more mindful of what you do *and* how you do it. You'll consider what you read, watch on television, listen to on the radio, and hear from others. You'll give more consideration to who takes up your child's time, and how and where and why.

Throw away the notion that children only learn while sitting behind a desk, and you see that at the same time they pick up reading, writing, and arithmetic, they also pick up attitudes, values, and behaviors. If your child hangs around with someone who curses all the time, you can easily figure out where he

EXPERIENCE

Scientists have confirmed what anyone who has ever watched a child grow already knows: Nature and nurture are inextricably intertwined. Nurture is that which the environment contributes to the whole that is any of us. The environment includes the influence of home and family and everything else that is a child's experience. Experience includes the emotions your child feels on the ball field, in church, and during time spent at grandma's house. It includes the programs he sees on television and movies and video games. It includes the messages he receives from books, peers, and elders, and dinner table conversations. It includes the influences of neighbors and relatives, clergy and teachers, best sibling and worst foe.

Experience includes every sight, touch, sniff, and sound. It includes every word, gesture, and emotion. It includes what goes on in the schoolyard, the bus, the classroom, and the locker room, in the friend's house, in the dark. It includes every birth we witness as well as every death. All of it becomes the experience that nurtures us as we grow. That nurture then becomes inextricably intertwined with our nature, that which is already inside us to be.

As our children's guides, we parents choose the nurture that is going to inextricably intertwine with the nature that is already inside our child. It is only right to put the quality of the nurture we provide at the top of our priority lists. Sometimes it seems we pay much more attention to that which nurtures children physically than to that which nurtures the whole person a child will become. Continual consumption of junk food is dangerous to a child's health. Continual consumption of junk experience is dangerous to who our child becomes.

(continues)

learned that four-letter word. Most of his other learning is taking place more subtly than his learning a four-letter word, however.

If your child spends large portions of time away from you and your positive outlook and influence, be extra vigilant about subtle negative influences. You need to consciously respond to them with your positive thoughts, words, and deeds. In return you'll find a child more supportive, interested, discerning, cooperative, and caring. These are the attitudes, values, and behaviors of a successful human being, including an academically successful one.

Money Doesn't Buy Academic Excellence Any More Than It Does Happiness

The price of public education rises every year because inside-the-box folks believe that dollars can fix education. Jump outside the box, and like other parents you learn that the price of educational success needn't be any more than what you have to spend. You don't need to mortgage your house to live the learning lifestyle.

If you can't or don't want to invest in fancy educational resources, don't worry; there is no need to do so. In fact, most

EDUCATIONAL MATERIALS
YOU ALREADY HAVE AROUND THE HOUSE

Material	Uses
Aluminum foil	You'll use it for everything
Analog and digital clocks	Telling time
Baking supplies	Arithmetic basics; home economic skills
Balloons and cork	Art and science projects
Beans	Counting; planting; dissecting; making pictures
Books	Information on a variety of subjects
Buttons	Sorting; making mosaics
Calculator	Arithmetic
Calendars	Basic time concepts
Computer programs	Edutainment
Contact Paper	Cheap lamination material
Crayons	Colorful art
Dice	Basic arithmetic skills; creating your own games
Food coloring	Learning about colors
Game spinners	Learning about probability
Graph paper and M&M's or other small colorful candies	Sorting; making graphs
Index cards	Making your own note cards, flash cards, games

(continues)

EDUCATIONAL MATERIALS
YOU ALREADY HAVE AROUND THE HOUSE
(continued)

Material	Uses
Internet connection	Accessing information
Library card	Key to a world of books
Math manipulatives (Lego bricks, milk jug lids, buttons, dry beans, M&M's as counters)	Arithmetic
Measuring cups and spoons	Studying fractions; multiplication, division, and more
Measuring tape (standard and metric)	Measuring
Note cards, paper, stamps, envelopes	Playing post office; writing
Paper	Writing; arts and crafts
Pencils	Writing
Puzzles	Great brain exercise
Real coins and bills	Understanding money; arithmetic skills
Recorded music	Appreciation; learning about styles; instruments; foreign countries
Ruler	Measuring
Salt dough ingredients	1,001 uses
Sidewalk chalk	Art; learning in the fresh air

Material	Uses
Small plastic containers from yogurt, ricotta cheese, etc.	Starting seeds; making a phone with string; storing manipulatives; studying shapes; arts and crafts
Straws	Arts and crafts
Tape	Holding things together

homeschoolers will tell you "real" things, like tools, money, calendars, gardens, bugs, and, as in the case of my granddaughter, golf clubs, are more valuable anyway. (Please see "Educational Materials You Already Have Around the House" for more ideas.) If you're the creative type, you and your child can craft much of the basic educational material. Not only will you save money, but the shared activity will result in creating products your child takes pride in. This increases the chances she'll use them again and again.

Once your family gets into the swing of the learning lifestyle, you'll all appreciate educational materials more than ever. Many families further keep down the cost by guiding friends and relatives to useful "edutainment" items when birthday and holiday gift-giving days roll around. "I know it sounds crazy, but my three kids really were happier to get a globe than a fire truck," rural West Virginia public school mom Cynthia Reynolds remembers. "We started this when the kids were little, but a couple of friends loved the idea so much they slowly guided their older children into the same direction with wonderful results."

You can set aside the idea that helping a child succeed in school is only for the privileged few. More necessary to success than money is your time, attention, and loving guidance—educational materials no amount of money can buy. Remember that the dollars you *do* spend on the learning lifestyle directly benefit your child's education. You get a lot of bang for the buck, and your child reaps the educational benefit directly.

PART TWO

Focus on: Your Unique Learner

"We seem, as a nation, to be drifting toward a new concept of childhood which says that a child can be brought into this world and allowed to fend for himself or herself. There is a disconnection here that demands our attention...a disconnection so pervasive between adult America and the children of America that we are all losing touch with one another."

RICHARD RILEY, *U.S. Secretary of Education, 1994*

CHAPTER 6

Put the Child Back into Childhood

I KNOW I'M DATING MYSELF, but here goes. I remember a time when preschool was almost unheard of and daycare wasn't a noun. Most families participated in "early years" homeschooling (although they didn't call it that) until somewhere around a child's fifth or sixth birthday. Until then we, all the neighborhood children, got together to ride bikes, visit each other's homes, and enjoy rainy day quiet time in our own rooms. Even after we began to go to school, we spent the summertime together chasing lightning bugs in our pajamas, creating impromptu ball games at the park, and enjoying cookies and Kool-Aid at a shaded picnic table in each other's backyards.

Fast-forward to life for children today, and the picture changes. For safety reasons, many of us wouldn't dream of sending our children out alone. Daycare is not just a noun but a necessity. Organized sports replace pickup teams. And because of an increasingly academic kindergarten, coupled with a decades' long push for preparedness, preschool has moved from a luxury to a prerequisite for school. Enter the availability of all those extracurricular activities, and the opportunity for a child to exercise her imagination disappears daily.

Many homeschoolers know the sting of criticism from loved ones and friends for what appears to be their relaxed attitude towards "school work," especially with elementary-school-aged children. Media critics relay fears that, spared the rigors of intense school-type study, these children will be unable to cope with higher education or the workplace. Despite such criticism, the families persist, secure in another lesson homeschooling has taught them about academic excellence: Kids thrive when loving adults put the "child" back into childhood.

The Child's Route to Academic Excellence

It all comes down to balance, really, the balance necessary for health and happiness. "When we place all the weight on one side of an airplane, it cannot soar smoothly," I wrote in *The Art of Education*. "When we place all importance on a child's intellect, he cannot soar smoothly, either. We make his flight toward independence unnecessarily difficult and dangerous. If we shift the plane's weight, we achieve equilibrium. Only when we pay equal attention to all aspects of a child, when *we* value his hands and heart equally with his head, will he achieve symmetry. Then watch him fly!"

Many parents believe the route to academic excellence shouldn't necessarily resemble an expressway. If we put a child on the expressway through childhood, we forget she isn't just an intellectual tractor trailer roaming the earth. We provide messages, subconsciously or otherwise, that it's okay to neglect her need for equal amounts of emotional and psychological support, without which all the "head" success in the world doesn't matter.

Melissa Conrad learned this lesson the hard way when, in the course of four years, her "gifted" oldest child skipped a grade at

QUALITIES FOR LEARNING

With your guidance your youngster is learning life's most important lessons naturally—painlessly—carrying them always in her heart as well as her head.

But your child also brings much to the learning experience. These are the qualities of curiosity, imagination, creativity, inner peace, humor, artistry, self-motivation, and intuition, the qualities essential to true education. These are the qualities we admire (and, go on, admit it, we also envy) in our culture's artists.

As your child grows, she can use these qualities in all areas of life during all moments of life, thus transforming each activity into learning, wherever she happens to be, whatever she happens to do, with whomever she happens to do it. The real world becomes her very teacher. Think of the possibilities for the greater community when more and more members of the human family bring these positive qualities into their lives.

All children need time to exercise their inherent characteristics if they are to grow and thrive. When you take responsibility for your child's education, you can make sure a lot of sun shines on these qualities. It's easier than you might imagine. In fact, kids do it naturally—through play. Is your child's natural impulse to play coincidence? Or simply "the way it's supposed to be?"

Adapted from Linda Dobson, The Art of Education:
Reclaiming Your Family, Community and Self *(Holt Associates, 1997)*

school not once, but twice. "The first time we watched his stress level soar and did everything we could to ease it, but the second time," remembers Melissa, "all hell broke loose, I see now, because while he was more than ready for the academic part, he wasn't nearly as advanced as his classmates socially and emotionally. We were in a real catch-22: We couldn't let the problem continue, and we couldn't move him back a grade or two, either. You might say we had no choice but to begin homeschooling him to give him the time, space, and experiences he needed to stay in balance."

The route to academic excellence looks a lot like a country road replete with interesting turns and detours that befit a child's natural curiosity and continuous need for new experiences. If we take this road, we guarantee that all necessary aspects of a child's education, those of head, heart, and hands, receive the attention required for wholeness.

The Magic of Childhood

Have you noticed? Clothes on the racks in the little girls department look like a miniature prostitute's Saturday night outfit. Music videos leave nothing about sex to the imagination. One of the nation's most popular video games puts the player in the role of a revengeful drug dealer complete with baseball bat and Uzi and a blood trail to track his victim. Young teens engage in oral sex because, hey, it isn't *really* sex. The hurry-up-and-grow-up message permeates every cultural nook and cranny.

Disturbing consequences come to the surface almost daily. One way to keep up with news like this is to go to Jimmy Kilpatrick's online *Education News,* a source that gives leads to newspaper articles. One such article is Andrew Julien's December 15, 2002, story in Connecticut's *Hartford Courant* titled "The Kids Are Hurting."

Julien's report should give us pause. "Gripped by depression and anxiety," he writes, "adolescents are swamping psychiatric wards and therapists' offices across the country." He goes on to say, "This stressed-out generation of American youth is caught in a double bind: intensifying pressure to meet an ever higher standard of success, and waning support and comfort within their families." The titles of the follow-up articles in his series tell the rest of the tale: "Parents Turn Up the Heat," "A Culture of Cruelty," and "Whatever Happened to Dinner?"

Among many sobering facts, Julien reports that the number of four- to fifteen-year-olds with psychiatric problems nearly tripled between 1979 and 1996, according to *Pediatrics, 2000.* Four year olds!

The best way to help our children keep the magic of childhood is to remember what they miss if they join the stampede to adulthood. Ironically, by racing to be the best and brightest, they bypass the development of some of the traits that make them efficient learners.

In a series of books published by Prima Publishing, three authors surveyed homeschooling parents to find out what they saw as their children's greatest learning assets as a result of homeschooling. The books are: *Homeschooling: The Early Years* (three- to eight-year-olds); *Homeschooling: The Middle Years* (eight- to twelve-year-olds); and *Homeschooling: The Teen Years* (thirteen- to eighteen-year-olds). The parents' answers were:

ASSETS OF THE EARLY YEARS

- Curiosity

- Imagination

- Enthusiasm

- Innocence/sense of wonder

- Pure love and joy

ASSETS OF THE MIDDLE YEARS

- Curiosity

- Independence and capability

- Perseverance

- Justice and fair play

- Compassion and kindness

ASSETS OF THE TEEN YEARS

- Explore interests

- Initiative and networking

- Self-direction

- Develop values

- Independence

You don't have to sit down and "teach" these learning assets to your children. Rather, you should develop—then nurture—them by allowing each child to "give up the things of childhood" in her own way and time. If you guard against cultural influences that may rush your child, you may see a youngster hanging on to stuffed animals longer than his friends or building with Legos long after his peers have given them up. I often wondered how big my son would get before he gave up snuggling with me on the couch in the evenings. One night, as a nine-year-old, he just stopped. It's a wise parent who allows her children to give up the things of childhood in their own time. The assets seem to stick better when childhood lasts longer.

By being patient, you can help your child hold onto the qualities that keep him excited, motivated, and creative. Here are some thoughts to help put the "child" back into childhood.

Children Are Wonderful

"One of the most important lessons homeschooling taught me is that kids are wonderful and easier to get along with than we've been led to believe," reports Elizabeth McCullough, a homeschooling mom of an eight-year-old and a twelve-year-old who

THOUGHTS TO HELP PUT THE "CHILD" BACK INTO CHILDHOOD

- Children are wonderful
- Children's gifts are easily destroyed
- Children need activity—and nothingness—for their own sake
- There is such a thing as "kid time"
- Honor privacy
- Actively protect your child's right to remain a child

works part-time. She admits childrearing is difficult and time-consuming, but she adds, "It's also delightful and challenging." Bad days are a matter of course for every family, so Elizabeth chooses to focus on the good times that she will always remember and treasure.

Key to appreciating and supporting your youngster as-is is to spend as much time as possible interacting with her above and beyond the hectic routine of daily life. Just think how you get to know a coworker best during breaks or before and after work, not while you're in the heat of completing an assignment or meeting a deadline. Similarly, you need relaxed circumstances to get to know your child as a person. Fortunately, most children, when feeling safe and secure in their environment, eagerly share what's on their minds. To help insure this occurs during your interactions, "Please don't buy into the popular culture's constant refrain that kids are a pain in the neck," Elizabeth advises. "This is the only childhood your children ever have, and the only one you'll ever get to spend with them."

If, Elizabeth adds, "your child really is a pain in the neck, meditate on why that might be so. Are you impatient with her? Does she misbehave? Is she tired or stressed? Are you dictating the agenda too much? Are your expectations out of whack? If so, once you understand the cause, you can do something about it."

Children's Gifts Are Easily Destroyed

The qualities that homeschooling parents notice in their children, from curiosity to enthusiasm, from perseverance to self-direction, are gifts that children who grow up with the type of respect I stress in this book possess inside. It's vital to allow these gifts the space and time to emerge. Indeed, if you trace the Latin root of the word "educate," you are led to a gold mine of meaning that could change your thinking about learning forever. Although we typically think that we receive an education by having knowledge "put in," that wasn't always so. The original meaning of the word *educere* was "to lead out."

Parents who act as learning guides have found this "opposite" approach to education creates the results they desire for their children. How we lost sight of this reality about learning has been examined in many books, but that isn't the purpose of *this* book. If you understand and take advantage of this "leading out" approach, you can apply this knowledge to every aspect of your family life.

No scale exists to measure our children's greatest gifts: curiosity, imagination, a sense of justice, and compassion. Alfie Kohn's *Punished by Rewards: The Trouble with Gold Stars, Incentive Plans, A's, Praise, and Other Bribes* was published in 1993. In it, the prolific author and speaker on human behavior, education, and social theory stated: "The evidence strongly suggests that tighter standards, additional testing, tougher grading, or more incentives will do more harm than good." Unfortunately, the No Child Left Behind Act, which incorporates all of this pressure—and more—was enacted eight years later in 2001.

The cultural pressure doesn't end there. Often, it continues at home. In his December 2002 article titled "Parents Turn Up the Heat," *Hartford Courant* writer Andrew Julien shared this:

> Wanting the best for your kids is nothing new, but some parents today go too far.

In a world where children are increasingly desperate for refuge from a swirl of demands and expectations, experts say that too many moms and dads are turning up the pressure instead.

Even with the best of intentions, some parents end up defining their own success in terms of the achievement of their children—in school, in sports, and on the social scene.

Others get caught up in chasing wealth and status, showering children with all the good things privilege has to offer, except the simple gifts of time and attention.

And, many parents get so wrapped up in the quest to create the perfect twenty-first century vision of an enriching childhood that they go to extremes in managing their children's lives.

Add it all together and you have children who are indulged, but in all the wrong ways, children who are driven to meet higher and higher visions of perfection, children who can end up despondent, frustrated or bitter.

"The world, as it is, has made it incredibly difficult for parents to care for their children," said Jean Adnopoz, an associate professor in the Child Study Center at Yale University School of Medicine. "It is a culture of excitement, of pleasure, of satisfaction, that keeps people running and chasing after something. But they often don't know what they are chasing—so they enlist their children in the chase."

When circumstances like these exist in a child's life, how can curiosity, innocence and wonder, compassion and kindness, self-direction and independence flourish? Recognize, nourish, and protect, to the best of your ability, these qualities in your child. She'll be happier and, by default, more successful.

Children Need Activity—and Nothingness—for Their Own Sake

Yes, some homeschooling parents put this cultural pressure on their children from the miniature classrooms in their homes.

Others, however, have learned that success also follows large doses of activity with no ulterior motive, that is, doing something for the sheer joy of the doing, period. For most children, sheer joy doesn't come from doing worksheets or term papers!

You might also try megadoses of nothingness, known in the old days as unscheduled, unfettered "free" time. "I began home-schooling by scheduling my son's entire day," says Oklahoma's Marcy Worth. "All the activities and books were so educational and I didn't want him to miss out on anything. Thank goodness for my friend Nancy who slowly but steadily showed me how to lighten up and give my son the chance to 'just be.'" Within the first few months of relatively free afternoons, "he discovered a talent for writing science fiction and a hunger to know anything and everything about law enforcement," Marcy recalls. "I guess it's no coincidence that today he's studying criminal justice in college."

People who are creating learning lifestyles have found that it's *good* for children to experience boredom from time to time. They've discovered that some of their children's greatest creativity arises during the moments no one is telling them what, when, or how to do something. As a bonus, children will usually turn to a favored activity or topic, providing you with clues as to where their interests lie.

Children being the active, energetic creatures they are gravitate toward play to fill unscheduled time. Learning guides, convinced that play is a child's most important work, will bend over backwards to ensure free time. Play is so vital to a child's ultimate success that Ann Lahrson Fisher devoted the first six chapters of *Fundamentals of Homeschooling* to play, considering it a habit of homeschooling along with conversations, togetherness, and growing up.

Play, Ann explains, gives children a sense of timelessness, power and control, and a creative outlet for self-expression. In addition, play provides the chance to imitate and practice life skills and allows time for the processing of new knowledge. "Play is so much more than a critically important element of learning," Ann says. "Play *is* learning! If play is learning in the early years, learning can be play in the later years. Learning *is* play!"

I know this may be a hard concept to grasp. I know it goes against almost everything we've been told and/or likely experienced in our own educational history. But "down time" makes sense, even more so today in an academic climate filled with "a swirl of demands and expectations" greater than we parents ever experienced in school. Your child's mental and emotional health is just as important as her physical health, not only for success in school but also for her desire to do well in the first place.

There Is Such a Thing As "Kid Time"

Simply watching children reveals a lot about them, their talents, idiosyncrasies, likes, and dislikes. You can also find out that children are as variable in their preferences for "awake" time as adults are. Even though your child must maintain the school's schedule, you will want to figure out when her "alert" time occurs and do what you can to "go with" her natural inclinations. Use this knowledge to plan activities at the time she's more likely to be attentive and involved. Homework or test review may flow more smoothly before school for the morning bird, or last thing before bed for the night owl.

Recent research also suggests that the rhythm of "kid time" is a lot different than our own. Not only do children need more sleep in general; scientists worry about "ill-timed sleep," mostly in the lives of teens. When your teenaged child tells you he can't go to bed because he won't get to sleep—or he can't wake up in the morning—the reason could very well be biological.

Teens are "biologically programmed to stay up later and wake up later than preteens," claims E. P. Bradley Hospital and Brown University School of Medicine's professor of psychology Mary Carskadon. So, with a need for at least eight hours of sleep each night, if your teen goes to bed at, say, midnight, then awakens to the alarm at six A.M., he's rising in the middle of his "biological night" (which certainly explains why everyone looks like a zombie in high school's first period math class). Their eyes may be open, but evidence suggests teens' bodies don't wake up until about eight A.M. Carskadon is on a crusade to get high schools to delay starting times so that teens have a fighting chance to be awake when the first bell rings.

If you research this topic in more depth and gather pertinent information, you might be able to persuade other parents to join in a campaign to request that the school honor the children's biological clocks. This will help not only your own child but all the children at the school.

Honor Privacy

In a world of easily accessible drugs and alcohol, sex and pornography, weapons and "bad influence" peers, honoring a child's privacy stands among a parent's greatest challenges. You'll find the task grows easier to accomplish as you spend more time talking, playing, and learning with your child. The reason is simple: The more you talk, play, and learn, the better you'll know each other, and the better you know each other, the more you'll trust each other. It's exactly the same with your child as with every other relationship you have.

A sense of privacy is vital to mental and emotional health. After a hard day's work, you look forward to the relative peace and sanctity of "your castle" for necessary "down time"—to read, listen to music, watch television, work on hobbies. Privacy is a "place" where you may let go of others' demands and be yourself. Even though your child may not be inclined to take time for herself or to understand its necessity, she, too, needs "a castle" where she can be herself.

Your child's daily pressures are almost certainly different than yours (she's not worrying about paying the mortgage or the rising cost of health care), but they're equally draining of her physical, mental, and emotional reserves. She, too, must spend a sizeable portion of her day "being on," whether that involves living up to others' expectations, meeting deadlines, fitting in, or figuring out what in the world the teacher wants. She, too, needs the opportunity to let her hair down and be herself in a place she knows is safe and secure—home. Only through ample opportunity to be herself will she learn to know and like herself. A prerequisite to academic excellence is to know who it is doing the learning!

Sylvia Mussaw well understands how difficult it is to honor a child's privacy at a time when you hear news reports about teenagers building bombs in their bedrooms. "First," says Sylvia, "we realized there's a difference between privacy for health's sake, and privacy to hide something. We focused on the former, which helped eliminate the latter. Preventive measures included plenty of televisions and telephones available, just not in bedrooms, and we kept the computer in the middle of the living room."

Sylvia knows these measures didn't totally remove the possibility of drugs or other detrimental materials finding their way into her children's lives, "but we talked so frequently and I knew them so well I would have noticed a change in behavior. My husband and I knew their friends and their typical schedules, and we knew they had plenty of positive reasons to take private time."

A personal space provides even more privacy. For younger children, this is where they can exercise imagination and creativity—to pretend—without interruption or ridicule. For older children, it's home to valued possessions, a place where they can exercise creative energy, and a sanctuary from younger siblings. For all, it's a place to read, write, think, dream, and plan.

Finally, honoring your child's privacy says you trust and respect him. I can't say it enough, that by living with trust and respect, a child develops trust and respect for others. Not a bad return for simply talking, playing, and learning together.

Actively Protect Your Child's Right to Remain a Child

The pressure on you, in the name of your child, comes from all sides—from the school to perform, from friends to keep up, from relatives to be the best. Just a couple of stories from coworkers about their children's successes in music or sports can send you looking for a bottle of your favorite libation, so certain are you that your child is scarred for life because he wouldn't know a sonata if he tripped over one and he's acquainted with a soccer ball because tripping over it is what he does best.

Not to worry. The next time a coworker regales you with tales of glory, smile and politely say, "That's wonderful. My husband (wife) and I hope for such things some time. Right now, we're having so much fun making sure Johnny (or Jill) reaps all the benefits of the only childhood he (or she) will have. I don't know where we'd find the time!" Such a comment will help quell your doubts about your offspring at the same time it spreads the idea among other parents that maybe, just maybe, the world would be a better place if children had more time to run, jump, giggle, and dream.

For Laura Tichenor, whose twin girls, now sixteen years old, "have tried every single educational method known to mankind," the greatest pressure came from her own mom. "We're nothing if not a family of achievers," says Lauri, "and it bothered Mom to no end that my girls were still happy playing with Barbies, climbing trees, and loving their stuffed animals after their twelfth birthday. It caused a few hard feelings when my husband and I defended their right to be children for as long as they felt necessary," Lauri recalls, "but I knew they were happy, well-adjusted, and growing according to their own timetable, which was the most important thing."

With so much pressure for your child to get on that cultural expressway, it's up to you to actively protect his right to remain a child. It's not the easiest task in the world, but neither is it impossible. The essential avenue to success is to recondition everyone who is in a position to hurry, push, or otherwise pressure your child. Yes, this means teachers and school administrators, but it also includes friends, relatives, neighbors, and even siblings who love to tease. Reconditioning these folks consists of a calm discussion of the opportunities and benefits available to your child through the learning lifestyle. Most people enjoy helping once they understand your goal, so offer concrete suggestions for what they might do. Of course these suggestions will vary among children, families, and circumstances, but here are a few ways all adults can start helping.

- Watch for newspaper and magazine articles, television programs, or videos that address the child's interests and share them

- Volunteer to take the child on relaxed tours of museums, zoos, and historic sites

- Take walks to the city park or hike through the country woods

- Arrange for and accompany your child on visits to everything from the glass factory to the pumpkin farm

- Create a game night or craft night and allow your child to choose the game or craft

- Take the child swimming, bowling, roller-skating, ice skating, or miniature golfing followed by an ice-cream sundae

- Recommend the books you enjoyed reading when you were your child's age; they may still be available. Look for them at the library during your regular visits

- Ask for recommendations of how your child can complete as much work as possible during regular school hours to free up "spare" time at home

LEARN MORE ABOUT THE SERIOUS BUSINESS OF PLAY

Dobson, Linda. *The Ultimate Book of Homeschooling Ideas: 500+ Fun and Creative Learning Activities for Kids Ages 3–12.* Prima Publishing/Random House, 2002.

Elkind, David. *The Hurried Child.* Addison-Wesley, 1981.

Engelhardt, Anne, and Cheryl Sullivan. *Playful Learning: An Alternate Approach to Preschool.* La Leche League International, 1986.

Jenkinson, Sally. *The Genius of Play: Celebrating the Spirit of Childhood.* Hawthorn Press, 2002.

Kaye, Peggy. *Games for Learning: Ten Minutes a Day to Help Your Child Do Well in School.* Noonday Press/Farrar Straus and Giroux, 1991.

Weston, Denise Chapman, and Mark S. Weston. *Playwise: 365 Fun-Filled Activities for Building Character, Conscience, and Emotional Intelligence in Children.* Jeremy P. Tarcher/Putnam Books, 1996.

- When you find a particularly interesting, compelling, or enjoyable activity, turn it into a tradition, something you do on that same day every year

With understanding and loving support on your side, you will see noticeable, positive changes in your child as time goes on. Don't be surprised when soon your lonely voice pleading for active protection of childhood becomes a chorus among your friends and family.

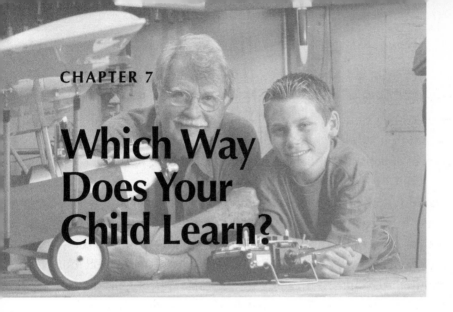

CHAPTER 7

Which Way Does Your Child Learn?

WHICH IS BETTER, a hammer, drill, or screwdriver?

Each tool is capable of "getting the job done," but not the same jobs in the same way. The tools are equally valuable—but different. Any job gets done quicker and more efficiently when we understand, accept, and work with the nature of the tool.

Figuring out how your child learns best is what this chapter is all about. As his learning guide, you will need to understand, accept, and work with his natural abilities. Because of the structure of education and classroom environment—large numbers of children and a finite amount of time—school instruction will suit the natural abilities of some children, but not all. If the structure works for your child, great. If it doesn't work (or maybe hinders learning), you will want to use other ways to help her learn at home.

Please allow me one more analogy for, as we talk about learning styles, it's important to keep healthy balance in mind. When a child isn't hungry, do we insist she eat anyway, using our role as an authoritative adult in her life to force unwanted food down her throat?

We wouldn't dream of doing such a thing! Instead, we'd likely ask how she feels, find out about her day, and check for a temperature. Then we'd watch for any other clues as to why she doesn't want to eat, all the while trusting that her body's innate response, lack of appetite, is probably a sign that something is wrong.

Odd, isn't it? As understanding, intelligent adults we wouldn't force-feed a child's belly, yet so often we find it relatively easy—and entirely justified—to force-feed her mind. Our society perpetuates the message that learning is—and must be— a difficult, if not downright ugly, experience. We expect our children to dislike it. Breaking through this stereotypical image, homeschoolers have found that lack of appetite for learning, just as for food, is not "normal" and likely a sign that something is wrong.

Figuring out which way your child learns, then, serves two important purposes. First, you give your child the chance to experience success through exercising her natural abilities. Second, by feeding her "food for the mind" that she likes and chooses for herself, she can rediscover the joy of learning.

First, Some Basics

Some very basic truths about learning are often overlooked. Putting them under a spotlight will help you to remember these truths as you go about learning in your home.

CHILDREN RISE TO CHALLENGES

If your child has lost touch with the joy of learning, quite possibly it's because of what has been termed the "dumbing down" of curriculum. To see what history tells us children are capable of, here is a copy of the eighth-grade final exam given in 1895 in Salina, Kansas, a representative, typical American town then and now. Keep in mind the test takers were of our grandparents' and great-grandparents' generations.

THE GOOD OL' DAYS—
EIGHTH GRADE IN 1895

This is the eighth-grade final exam given in 1895 in Salina, Kansas. It was taken from the original document on file at the Smoky Valley Genealogical Society and Library in Salina, Kansas, and reprinted by the *Salina Journal.*

Grammar (Time, 1 hour)

Give nine rules for the use of Capital Letters.

Name the Parts of Speech and define those that have no modifications.

Define Verse, Stanza and Paragraph.

What are the Principal Parts of a verb? Give Principal Parts of do, lie, lay and run.

Define Case. Illustrate each Case.

What is Punctuation? Give rules for principal marks of Punctuation.

Write a composition of about 150 words and show therein that you understand the practical use of the rules of grammar.

Arithmetic (Time, 1.25 hours)

Name and define the Fundamental Rules of Arithmetic.

A wagon box is 2 ft. deep, 10 ft. long, and 3 ft. wide. How many bushels of wheat will it hold?

If a load of wheat weighs 3942 lbs., what is it worth at 50 cts. per bu., deducting 1050 lbs. for tare?

District No. 33 has a valuation of $35,000. What is the necessary levy to carry on a school seven months at $50 per month, and have $104 for incidentals?

Find cost of 6720 lbs. coal at $6.00 per ton.

(continues)

THE GOOD OL' DAYS *(continued)*

Find the interest of $512.60 for 8 months and 18 days at 7 percent.

What is the cost of 40 boards 12 inches wide and 16 ft. long at $20 per m?

Find bank discount on $300 for 90 days (no grace) at 10 percent.

What is the cost of a square farm at $15 per acre, the distance around which is 640 rods?

Write a Bank Check, a Promissory Note, and a Receipt.

U.S. History (Time, 45 minutes)

Give the epochs into which U.S. History is divided.

Give an account of the discovery of America by Columbus.

Relate the causes and results of the Revolutionary War.

Show the territorial growth of the United States.

Tell what you can of the history of Kansas.

Describe three of the most prominent battles of the Rebellion.

Who were the following: Morse, Whitney, Fulton, Bell, Lincoln, Penn, and Howe?

Name events connected with the following dates: 1607, 1620, 1800, 1849, and 1865.

Orthography (Time, 1 hour)

What is meant by the following: Alphabet, phonetic orthography, etymology, syllabication?

What are elementary sounds? How classified?

What are the following, and give examples of each: Trigraph, subvocals, diphthong, cognate letters, linguals?

Give four substitutes for caret 'u'.

Give two rules for spelling words with final 'e'. Name two exceptions under each rule.

Give two uses of silent letters in spelling. Illustrate each.

Define the following prefixes and use in connection with a word: Bi, dis, mis, pre, semi, post, non, inter, mono, super.

Mark diacritically and divide into syllables the following, and name the sign that indicates the sound: Card, ball, mercy, sir, odd, cell, rise, blood, fare, last.

Use the following correctly in sentences, Cite, site, sight, fane, fain, feign, vane, vain, vein, raze, raise, rays.

Write 10 words frequently mispronounced and indicate pronunciation by use of diacritical marks and by syllabication.

Geography (Time, 1 hour)

What is climate? Upon what does climate depend?

How do you account for the extremes of climate in Kansas?

Of what use are rivers? Of what use is the ocean?

Describe the mountains of North America.

Name and describe the following: Monrovia, Odessa, Denver, Manitoba, Hecla, Yukon, St. Helena, Juan Fernandez, Aspinwall and Orinoco.

Name and locate the principal trade centers of the U.S.

Name all the republics of Europe and give capital of each.

Why is the Atlantic Coast colder than the Pacific in the same latitude?

(continues)

Describe the process by which the water of the ocean returns to the sources of rivers.

Describe the movements of the earth. Give inclination of the earth.

Children need the opportunity to experience real success. They know when they aren't being challenged and when there is nothing to rise to. Highly acclaimed teacher Marva Collins, whose motto for her teacher training workshops is "Every child is a born achiever," put this knowledge to work in the small private school she founded years ago, as well as in the Chicago public schools where she was a classroom teacher.

Marva threw out the "See Spot go" books and introduced her students to Shakespeare, Sophocles, and Tolstoy, explains Anthony Robbins in *Awaken the Giant Within* (Fireside, 1993). Even though her fellow teachers were sure the students wouldn't understand any of it, Marva's students thrived on it.

Why? "Because she believed so fervently in the uniqueness of each child's spirit," explains Robbins, "and his or her ability to learn anything. She communicated with so much congruency and love that she literally got them to believe in themselves— some of them for the first time in their young lives."

DIFFERENT CHILDREN = DIFFERENT RATES OF LEARNING

When we understand that all children are different and that they gravitate toward different learning styles, we can take the next logical step—educationally speaking—and see that they will learn at different rates. By allowing their children to learn at the pace they themselves dictate, homeschooling parents often find "inconsistencies" among their children. One sibling is ready to read at age four, while another may not read until age ten. (Incidentally, most parents report that when both children become teenyboppers, no one can tell which was reading earliest.)

In addition, the same child may display disparities as he goes about learning. It's not unusual to find an eight-year-old who reads at fourth-grade level, solves math problems at sixth-grade level, and understands science at a second-grade level. As Ann Lahrson Fisher, homeschooling author and former public and private school teacher, describes it, "Many children in any given school group will not be thriving at any particular moment."

Knowing this, you can display that patience and understanding toward your children that so many folks admire in their homeschooling counterparts. You will accept where your child currently is and start the learning journey there. It's less stressful, more effective, and much more realistic.

CHILDREN NEED ONE-ON-ONE TIME

Imagine if you went to work day after day, year after year, and at no time did anyone comment on how well you were doing. Or imagine always seeing your spouse in a group setting, never just the two of you alone.

We humans require the intimacy of one-on-one contact with others throughout our lives, including going to school. "Some children who thrive in one-on-one situations get lost in larger group settings, and I include both social and academic settings here," says Ann Lahrson Fisher.

If your child feels lost in the larger setting (and if you don't know, go ahead and find out), he will appreciate learning in a one-on-one situation at home. It is essential to his well-being, as well as to his educational success. For this child, family-centered education can become the highlight of his day.

The Beginner's Guide to Learning Styles

I highly recommend you borrow or preferably, buy, for your constant reference two primers on learning styles: *In Their Own Way: Discovering and Encouraging Your Child's Personal Learning Style* by Thomas Armstrong, Ph.D. (Jeremy P. Tarcher, 1987) and *Discover Your Child's Learning Style* by Mariaemma Willis and Victoria Kindle Hodson (Prima Publishing, 1999).

EIGHT WAYS TO BLOOM

Thomas Armstrong was a learning disabilities specialist who one day upped and quit his job. Armstrong's personal experience had convinced him there were no such things as learning disabilities. Instead of disabilities, Armstrong saw "unique learning styles that the schools didn't clearly understand." He happened upon Harvard psychologist Howard Gardner's theory of multiple intelligences, which supported his observations. Armstrong made the information part of his classic book, making the theory practical and accessible for parents and others. (Gardner added an eighth intelligence to the list in 1996.)

Read the sidebar, "Howard Gardner's Multiple Intelligences," and keep your child in mind. Armstrong notes that all children possess all the intelligences, although not in the same proportions. He cautions, "Resist the temptation to categorize your child into one of the intelligence groups. You should find your child described in several of the sections. Take what seems to apply to your child in these descriptions and add to this other observed strengths and weaknesses in all varieties of intelligence. Taken together, these constitute your child's personal learning style."

HOWARD GARDNER'S MULTIPLE INTELLIGENCES

- Linguistic: Your child thinks in words; possesses good auditory skills; learns best by verbalizing or hearing and seeing words

- Logical-Mathematical: Your child thinks conceptually; enjoys patterns and experimenting

- Bodily-Kinesthetic: Your child processes knowledge through bodily sensations; possesses fine motor coordination; learns by moving or acting things out

- Visual-Spatial: Your child thinks in images and pictures; is inventive and/or artistic

- Musical: Your child possesses high appreciation of music or a talent for creating, including singing; hears sounds that others don't; is sensitive to nonverbal sounds

- Interpersonal: Your child is good at organizing and communicating (or negatively, manipulating); natural mediator; learns best by relating and cooperating

- Intrapersonal: Your child possesses deep awareness of inner feelings and ideas; has deep sense of self; shows qualities of inner wisdom or intuition

- (Added in 1996) Naturalist: Your child is skilled at observing, understanding, and organizing patterns in the natural environment; is a good classifier; analyzes minute differences, as in sounds of different engines or fingerprint variations

In the list you will notice an important detail. Of the eight intelligences, only the first two are typically addressed in classrooms. A full 75 percent are not addressed and, often, little appreciated. In fact, looking at the different intelligences in this way, we can assume the odds favor trouble more than they do success.

If you don't know the intelligences that are strongest in your child, let him read the list and give you leads. To determine the strengths of younger children, you can ask questions based on the list. Whatever your child's age, remember to observe, observe, observe, because, as with so much of this business of helping your child succeed, the answers are right under your nose (courtesy of your child himself!) if you know what to look for.

WHAT TO LOOK FOR

Identifying your child's intelligences isn't rocket science. You don't need a degree in teaching or anything else. You just need to talk with your child and watch what she naturally shows you. Let's look at a few make-believe children to see what information they give us.

Susie

At six years old, Susie enjoys playing by herself just as much as, if not more than, with other children. During solo time her play is imaginative, well-thought-out, and often artistic. Others say she's quiet, but she talks with her mom about everything, leaving mom wondering how in the world such a small child could have such deep thoughts. Susie can often be heard singing softly to her dolls or pretending to read to them.

Susie leans heavily toward intrapersonal intelligence, with a dose of musical on the side. With her inclination toward the artistic, quite possibly she's a visual learner, thinking in images and pictures.

Johnny

Johnny's grandma calls him "Dennis the Menace." Always on the go, eight-year-old Johnny loves all sports equally and is happy playing King of the Mountain with his many friends way past dinnertime. His teacher says he never sits still in class; she's worried about possible Attention Deficit Hyperactivity Disorder, in part because he's always more interested in talking with his friends than doing his lessons. Johnny does well with arithmetic, but, oh, his spelling and reading are way below grade level.

Like so many little boys, Johnny makes sense of the world with his body and senses (Bodily-Kinesthetic). He's a conceptual thinker who finds arithmetic fundamentals easy to grasp. He's got great interpersonal intelligence.

Sally

Sally's mom swears her child was born reading. At ten years of age, Sally either reads herself to sleep each night, listens to a good book on tape, or still enjoys being read to by her mother. She keeps her book and tape collections meticulously organized.

Sally has kept a journal since she was old enough to write. In it she keeps track of everything she discovers during nature walks, camping trips, or observations she makes during all the free time she spends in the backyard. If family members have questions about birds, butterflies, or which flowers bloom when, they know they have a walking encyclopedia in the house. Her few close friends share her interest.

Sally's interest in nature reveals her naturalist intelligence. She's more intrapersonally aware than interpersonally. It's a good bet Sally thinks in words and learns best by hearing and seeing words (Linguistic learner).

Educational Profiling

As you figure out your child's intelligences, start putting to work all the background information you possess about your child. In *Discover Your Child's Learning Style,* educators Willis and Kindle Hodson have created a do-it-yourself workbook for parents of children six years of age and older. They recommend parents and child get together and examine five aspects of educational enhancement: dispositions, talents, interests, modality, and environment. See the Learning Style Profile for details.

Additionally, *Discover Your Child's Learning Style* supplies worksheets that help you and your child pinpoint useful changes/activities/additions/subtractions you can make at home to improve your child's performance in school. The authors include suggestions to aid you in creating goals and sharing your discoveries with your child's teacher. They also walk you through two sample profiles and suggest that you take the profile, too—an exercise that is well worth the small amount of time it takes.

THE BENEFIT OF SELF-PROFILING

Just as we don't all learn alike, we all don't think alike, either. As parents who want to help our children learn and grow, we have to put the brakes on our natural inclination to make judgments about our children's learning styles when they don't match our own disposition and preferences.

If you need quiet to study, you worry when your daughter prepares for a test with the radio blaring. If you love committee work, you can't understand why your son wants to work on the science project alone and not with his buddies. If you're a natural-born speller, you begin to think your atrocious speller is just lazy. If you prefer to read the directions first, you go crazy when your child plunges right into putting together the eight hundred pieces. (Mmm, maybe it would be good for all spouses to compare their profiles as a technique to increase marital bliss.)

"Differences" are not necessarily problems. Comparing your profile to your child's can end a lot of unnecessary conflict. Additionally, "You are able to move on to problem solving about what can be done to give your child the foundation he needs in math [for example]—staying focused on a solution rather than worrying or feeling frustrated," explain Willis and Kindle Hodson.

THE LEARNING STYLE PROFILE

Dispositions

Performing: Your child prefers activities that are entertaining, relevant, challenging, and hands-on. He learns best when teaching is short and to the point, allows movement, involves games, manipulatives, and audiovisuals

Producing: Your child prefers structure and order and the opportunity to organize. She learns best when teaching is logical and sequential and allows for planning, scheduling, and due dates

Inventing: Your child prefers experimental activity and the opportunity to question, design, and discover. He learns best when teaching is direct and provides "intellectual" ideas, theories, models, and time for exploration

Relating/Inspiring: Your child prefers social activity, incorporation of personal feelings, and the opportunity to interact. She learns best when teaching offers individualization, small groups, and cooperative interaction.

Thinking/Creative: Your child prefers activity that is creative and has artistic or philosophical aspects, provides artistic expression and opportunity to wonder, think, and dream. He learns best when teaching allows for time alone and involves the creative process.

Talents

(Note the similarities to Gardner's intelligences.)
Criteria to define talents are:

- Activities your child performs with ease

- She is ahead of her peers in areas where she has not received previous instruction

(continues)

THE LEARNING STYLE PROFILE *(continued)*

- His ability will be dormant, but not lost, if it doesn't get recognized and developed
- Her ability becomes apparent in activities not necessarily directly related

"Talents" include music, math-logic reasoning, mechanical reasoning, word-language reasoning; spatial; body coordination; interactive self, interactive others, interactive animals, interactive nature; humor, and life enhancement (the ability to add aesthetic value to the ordinary, every day routine).

Interests

The activities that your child chooses to pursue are valid expressions of his learning style, yet they

- Are often overlooked by parents
- Don't always match a child's talents
- Need to be observed

It helps if you assist your child in prioritizing her interests, both short-term and long-term.

Modality

Modality refers to the senses through which we take in information and process it. Modalities are the following:

- Auditory modality: Your child learns through listening or through talking and discussing
- Visual modality: Your child learns through pictures (charts, graphs, maps, etc.) or through print (reading and writing)

- Tactile-kinesthetic modality: Your child learns through touch or through movement

Environment

Do not ignore the understanding that different people learn best under different circumstances. Pay attention to these environmental differences:

- Sound: Your child prefers quiet or needs noise

- Body Position: Your child prefers to sit, recline, or stand

- Interaction: Your child prefers to be alone or with others, either quietly or interacting

- Lighting: Your child likes full-spectrum lighting better than fluorescent; dimmed lights have calming effect

- Temperature: Your child is uncomfortable when his environment is either too hot or too cold

- Food: Keep healthy food and drink available to increase your child's learning efficiency.

- Color: Remember that color can affect mood. Use colors to energize or soothe. Your child's favorite colors in her environment can contribute to positive thinking and motivation.

What to Do

For some parents, Howard Gardner's and Thomas Armstrong's way of looking at intelligences will resonate with their observations of their child. For others, Willis and Kindle Hodson's learning style profiles will make more sense. Still others will find a blend of both works best. Whichever way you figure out how your child learns, author Ann Lahrson Fisher's "Ways of Learning" takes you to the next step. Her suggested activities are good starting points for many of the different learning types.

Are you wondering, for example, how chants, songs, and rhymes as outlined under the Auditory way of learning will help your child in school? If she has to memorize state capitals for a test, or needs to remember the chief exports of Guatemala, make up a chant, song, or rhyme about the necessary facts and your auditory learner will have an easier time remembering.

How will your interpersonal learner pick up schoolworthy information through family discussion, you ask? By talking about what he needs to remember! This child will likely learn and retain more information during a half-hour conversation than he would by reading the same information alone for hours.

In key skill areas like reading and arithmetic, Lahrson Fisher advises you to go the extra mile and present the information in as many ways as you can think of. "When your child takes an interest in reading, for example," Ann begins, "be sure you read to her (auditory) and she can follow along in the book with you (visual). Point out phonetic symbols and how words are put together (interpretive). Explore letters and words using (tactile) materials such as magnetic letters, felt letters, tracing in sand trays, making cookies shaped like letters, and the like." Ann continues, "Help her write words, sentences, or stories and illustrate them using any art media of interest (self-expression/physical). Help her act out, illustrate, or retell stores (relational/physical). Make a point of using books and materials that are of particular interest to her (interpretive). Math-inclined children will enjoy counting words, pages, characters, illustrations, or other patterns of interest that they discover in the reading material. Get the idea?"

If not, Ann offers more advice: "Consider a child's early explorations of multiplication," she says. "Physical and tactile exploration might include manipulating a set of shells or stones

WAYS OF LEARNING

Auditory

External: verbal explanation; audio-books, tapes, videos, CDs, verbalization

Internal: self-talk, journaling

Rhythmic: music, rhythms, poetry, chants, songs, and rhymes

Visual

Observation

Demonstration

Example

Movies

Videos

Internet research

Photos and drawings

Models

Museums

Internal visualization

Books, including historical fiction, biographies

Physical Exploration

Trial and error

Sensory, through all the senses, including tactile and muscular

(continues)

WAYS OF LEARNING *(continued)*

Hands-on, manipulative tasks, such as cooking, woodwork, and sewing

Games and sports

All kinds of play

Practice or repetition

Field trips

Crafts

Construction

Self-Expression

Play

Visual arts

Crafts

Music

Creative writing

Speaking

Building

Fantasy

Mental

Visualization

Brainstorming

Memorizing and rote learning

Reflection and analysis

Divergent thinking

Convergent thinking

Mathematics and logic

Analytic writing

Relational (Interacting with Others or Self)

Dramatics: writing, attending, performing, or producing

Shared practice

Direct instruction from another

Indirect or casual instruction from another

Dialogue and debate

Group games and activities

Family discussions

Writing letters and journals

Making movies, Web sites, and videos

Interpretive

Reading: interpreting symbols of the spoken word to gain meaning

Math: interpreting symbols of number, including timelines, charts, and
graphs

Foreign language

Ann Lahrson Fisher

into arrays or grid patterns. Play games that use a game board, such as chess, that can demonstrate a math concept, such as rows and columns that can be counted in multiples."

"Does your child have an active imagination?" Ann asks. "Create a rich or silly image together—say, ballerinas in pink tutus on unicycles. Line them up in rows and columns in your mind's eye. Draw the image and then count the rows and columns. Story-loving children can build stories around the image; artistic children can draw or paint; musically talented children may create a marching band."

Is your child physically active? "Give him a problem like this," says Ann. "Can he hop on one foot for eight hops without stopping? How many hops would that be if he did this twice? Three times? What if he hopped three times in a row for eight times? Can he make up a problem of his own using a jump rope? Roller skates? A basketball? And so on. Give your active seat-work-resistant child these kinds of problems to solve and he'll soon think that doing math is one big party."

Finally, "An older child who understands multiplication but has trouble committing the facts to memory can benefit from fact practice through games, rote learning, chants, song, and the like. And," Ann adds, "make sure your child has a chance to learn through at least three different modes." (You can find out more about Ann's book at www.nettlepatch.net/homeschool.)

I sure hope you and your child are beginning to have a lot of fun, because that happens to be one of the upcoming "Six Principles of Successful Learning."

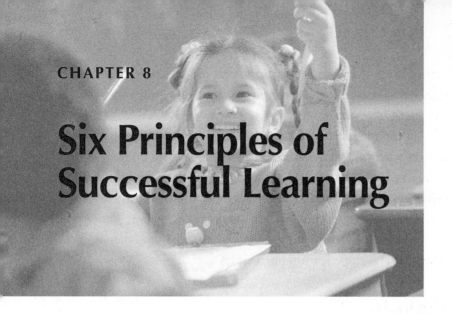

CHAPTER 8

Six Principles of Successful Learning

P LEASE GET A PEN AND PAPER, and sit down. Write a 1500-word paper about golf, on either its history or its rules. Be sure to watch your spelling and grammar because I intend to point out every error you make. Oh, and get it done within the next two days.

What's that? You had other plans for your time? You say you don't want to? What do you mean, you don't care about golf? I like golf, so I have decided that if you need some writing practice it won't kill you to write your paper about something I like. Why, I'm even allowing you choice—if you don't want to write about the history, write about the rules. See how open-minded I am?

How would you feel if I really did this? Angry? Insulted? Would you tell me to take a flying leap off a bridge before you go and do what you want to do? I would never have the nerve to say this to any adult, and if a friend said it to me, I'd be the first to offer her a ride to the highest bridge. Now let me ask the bottom-line questions. If I sincerely thought it was in your best interest to learn about golf, would writing a report about it get the job done? Might there be better ways to motivate you? I'm sure you can think of several.

Unfortunately, I can't afford to send you to the Bahamas for lessons with Mel Gibson. Keep this Bahamas idea on your "motivation to learn about golf" list, though, (change the location and celebrity to suit yourself) so you can see how such a trip fulfills several of the six principles of successful learning. Perhaps it might even turn you into a pro, a pro A+ parent, that is. Let's take a look at these learning principles.

Curiosity

The *American Heritage Dictionary of the English Language* gives this definition of curiosity and it is applicable to our purposes: "A desire to know or learn; especially about something new or strange." When we also look up "desire," we see that it's defined as "To wish or long for; want; crave."

Curiosity, then, is a longing for, wanting, craving to know or learn. Children are born curious. We all have witnessed our baby eager to become mobile, the toddler getting into everything humanly possible, and the three-year-old constantly asking, "Why?" Curiosity is one of the most important assets a child possesses. Parents who make their child's education a priority will want to protect his curiosity if it still exists and rekindle it if it has been extinguished. Rather than accept a decline in your child's curiosity as "natural" (which it surely is not), an A+ parent will vigilantly feed it and makes sure it gets lots of regular work.

NURTURING AND EXERCISING CURIOSITY

As the one who knows your child best, you will need to determine where he sits on the curiosity scale so you can figure out how much, if any, rekindling is necessary. Generally, younger children display more curiosity. For them, many life aspects are still interesting, and folks tend to be more patient with their questions. They haven't acquired a history of negative learning experiences, and they haven't yet learned through cultural cues that being smart isn't "cool." With older children, their track record in school may reveal how much natural curiosity they still have. Generally speaking, the more positive answers a child receives over the years, the more curiosity he will continue to show.

One of the most rewarding aspects for you as your child's learning guide is recognizing her need for certain information, then presenting the subject matter, especially at times when your child is less than thrilled. Here's where you get to reach into the bag of tricks you've learned so far and summon up your own creativity to help make the material significant to your reluctant child.

Once you pique your child's curiosity, it then flies on wings of its own. Like many other homeschooling parents, Rhode Island's Cathy McCarthy has become a piquing master. "The boys just didn't give a hoot about the Revolutionary War, and I now know I didn't make things any better when I insisted they sit down and 'read just three chapters' about it in a history textbook," says Cathy.

She stopped insisting and instead left the children's history magazine, *Cobblestone,* lying around with the cover story about a famous battle clearly visible. When the family went to the video store, Cathy exclaimed, "Oh, look, I'd really like to see *The Patriot* again." (Bonus for Mom: Mel's in it.)

"I actually went up into the attic and dug out a paper I wrote about the war in grade school, complete with misspellings, red marks, and a C– grade. The boys ate it up," Cathy says. "We visited an historical enactment in a town a few hours away, and I was ecstatic when the boys excitedly looked at the program for the next day and asked if we could go back. (We did.) The day after that we baked Johnnycake—it was terrific."

Want more? Ask the teacher for a list of educational television programs about the war. Visit Philadelphia. Spend an evening on the Internet gathering enough facts to play a Revolutionary War "Who Am I?" during dinner tomorrow night. Play "Going on a Bear Hunt" and only list objects or people that were around in 1775. Visit an historic cemetery during a full moon and see who can find the oldest tombstone. Leave an interesting history Web site open on your browser.

Not all of these activities will appeal to all children. Once you identify your child's learning style, you'll know the ones to try first.

Right about now you may be wondering how this is going to help your child get an A on the quiz tomorrow or the final exam at the end of the year. Here's how it works. Living the learning lifestyle means you and other family members understand that if one learning process is boring or isn't working, there are many others to try. You pique your child's curiosity, a task that grows easier and more fun with experience, because once you know how she learns, you can choose the approaches that will most likely work.

This is where curiosity grows its wings. I'm putting this sentence in bold print so you can easily find it again or, better yet, just memorize it. **Curiosity creates interest, interest increases attention to the task at hand, and attention gives rise to learning.**

Some lucky children perform well in school even though they're not that interested in the subject or even paying close attention. Often, these are the children who possess large amounts of linguistic and/or logical-mathematical intelligences. The good news is that schools often present information in such a way that these children easily assimilate it, even if only until they take the test. The bad news is that this group likely represents no more than 25 percent of the student population. The majority of children need information to be presented in other ways to achieve success. We need to pique their curiosity so that they become genuinely interested and attentive.

For curiosity to grow, it needs exercise—lots of it. Your focus on family-centered learning will provide many opportunities, to be sure. Remember, it's both the number of opportunities and the duration of each that counts. Let's liken it to physical exercise. You might think I'm really something if I tell you I work out every day. Will you be equally impressed when I add that I exercise for two minutes each day? (Darn. I didn't think so.)

As with physical exercise, curiosity exercise requires time. The best way to provide this time is to leave your curious child alone. Your child spends a large portion of her "work day" in an environment requiring constant shifting of gears. Even when she is enjoying the topic or experiment or discussion or art project or even the chance to write a test essay, she loses out when the period bell interrupts and she has to move on to her next class. It's like doing warm-up exercises and then quitting before the workout.

A child's curiosity receives the most exercise when she's allowed to pursue an activity and continue it until she finds her answers to the questions that inevitably arise. Yes, this may mean she spends hours building a Lego contraption, or leaves half-finished experiments all over the kitchen or bathroom. It may mean keeping an aquarium, or gathering the world's largest collection of seashells. It may mean your child buries his nose in comic books far past bedtime, or you hear more about basketball than you ever cared to know.

As pull-ups build arm muscles, free exploration strengthens curiosity. The former creates a strong body, the latter, a strong mind.

USING CURIOSITY AS A WINDOW ON YOUR CHILD'S MIND

The parent of a curious child is lucky, indeed, because she has a window on her child's mind. The interests you're observing and the questions you're answering help you recognize and assess your child's learning. They reveal the information he is gathering and working with at any particular moment.

For instance, your child's question to you might let you know she was listening to and comprehending the radio news report even as she seemed oblivious to it while doing her homework at the kitchen table. After you show him the math involved in figuring out baseball statistics (because he loves everything baseball), your son races to get the morning newspaper first. He wants to double-check the figures on how his favorite players performed last night. After you read a few of Laura Ingalls Wilder's novels together, your daughter asks why the family in the book made their own clothes instead of going to a store to buy them.

Man has not invented a test sufficient enough to uncover the workings of your child's mind anywhere nearly as accurately as your own open communication with your curious child.

Intrinsic Motivation

A large majority of homeschooled children use much of their time to learn about and participate in topics of personal interest. In many cases, these topics become the basis of a homeschooled child's adult career. Just ask Samantha Bouyea about her older son, Jason.

"Would you believe when he was eight years old I'd be awakened by noises coming from the kitchen," Samantha asks, "and at three o'clock in the morning come downstairs to find Jason concocting the recipe that just couldn't wait until morning? The first book he read cover to cover was a cookbook." As a teen, Jason wouldn't take a summer job unless it involved a kitchen, and at age seventeen he headed off to culinary school.

"He toured the finest restaurants in France and Italy and graduated with honors," says a proud Samantha. "Next month he opens the doors to his own restaurant."

Families across the country find that pursuit of knowledge motivated by interest offers children the freedom of mind and heart to discover that which is inside them: passions, fears, strengths, weaknesses, temperament, tolerance. In other words, at the same time she learns about a topic, a child learns much about herself, "leading out" that which is within, a true measure of educational achievement.

The pursuit of knowledge motivated by interest provides children the chance to learn at their own pace without fear of failure. Interest allows them to create, recognize, and follow up on opportunities. It becomes the gateway through which children go to develop the relevant skills they'll need as they advance toward independence.

ARE HOMESCHOOLING PARENTS LAZY?

A homeschooling friend jokes that she decided to homeschool her children because she was too lazy to get up in the morning to put them on the school bus. While it's true that many family-centered learning families are able to avoid the morning's mad dash, there is another reason why the outside world may think that homeschooling parents are lazy—some of them want their children to begin educating themselves as soon as possible. They achieve this most thoroughly and rapidly by cultivating their children's intrinsic motivation, the motivation that comes from within the child instead of from external factors.

It isn't that these homeschooling parents are really lazy. Rather they see their role in the learning lifestyle less as "teacher as dispenser of knowledge" and more as "creator of an environment that supports intrinsic motivation." Their function is different, but it is no less challenging and rewarding.

Path to Purpose

We need only recall our own school days to see how external forces of control permeated our experience. How frustrating this was! Consider this recent posting on a national homeschooling e-mail list: "Kids need purpose in their lives," wrote homeschooling mom Pam Sorooshian. "They are filled with purpose when they are young—everything they do, every move they make, has purpose.

Respectful and observant adults honor the purposes of little children. Some kids make school their purpose (as the adult world tells them they must), but many do not. By the time they reach their teens, many kids, most kids, have lost that sense of purpose—even many of those who originally made school their purpose have, by that time, lost interest in it (for all kinds of reasons).

"Ask a four-year-old, 'Why are you doing that?' and she will always have an answer.

"Ask a high school student, 'Why are you studying the French Revolution?'

"I asked this of my sixteen-year-old niece, an A student in the gifted program," Pam continues. "She answered, 'I don't know. I guess because of that old saying that if we don't remember history we're doomed to repeat it.'

"So I asked, 'Out of all the history of the world, why the French Revolution? What is important about it?' (She'd just spent six weeks studying about it for hours per day).

"She answered, 'I don't know, but I can tell you the headings of all six chapters on it.'

"I am serious; that is what she said! She'd been working on a 'report.' Her report had a section for each of the chapters in the book and the titles were what she remembered. I could get absolutely nothing out of her about why the French Revolution might be useful to know about."

Some historians contend that schools were created mainly to supply the Industrial Age with employees. "Schools had bells; factories had whistles," writes Daniel Pink in *Free Agent Nation: How America's New Independent Workers Are Transforming the Way We Live* (Warner Business Books, 2001). "Schools had report card grades; offices had pay grades. Pleasing your teacher prepared you for pleasing your boss. And," he adds, "in either place, if you achieved a minimal level of performance, you were promoted." The Industrial Age has come and gone, and most of our nation's other institutions have evolved into new roles. Yet schools, for the most part, have not kept up with the times. This lack of change is creating an educational irrelevance that makes it much more important for us as parents to create a learning lifestyle and sense of educational purpose at home.

Fun

For the sake of children everywhere, it's time to shatter the myth that learning isn't fun. This myth is so ingrained that schools come under parental fire when they try to lighten up and move toward individualized instruction. For a May 2001 article in the *Chicago Sun-Times,* education reporter Rosalind Rossi investigated the results of mixed-age classrooms that were mandated in the 1990 School Reform Act for Kentucky's primary grades. "For some parents, the thought of multiage classrooms is jarring," reports Rossi. The negative feelings persisted, even "though test scores were rising."

"It didn't look like learning was going on," explained Lisa Gross, a spokesperson for the Kentucky Department of Education. "It looked like kids were having a ball and it didn't resemble what parents were familiar with."

If homeschoolers had a dime for every time they've heard how they're ruining their children for the world of higher education or work, they'd all be hanging out with Bill Gates and Donald Trump. Since no one is offering dimes, they're content with the knowledge that allowing learning to remain fun, just as it is for a young child, continues to serve the needs of school-aged children.

Let's go back to golf for a moment. Even if you think it's the most boring game ever invented, if I say, "Hey, let's go play with Mel—in the Bahamas (or fill in your own names)," all of a sudden I've turned the boring into fun. Your desire—to learn about golf (right?)—just shot up a notch or three.

Contrary to popular opinion, anyone can make learning fun, especially someone who wants the learner to enjoy and reap lifetime benefits from the experience. Making it fun becomes especially important if the child needs an antidote to exposure to the myth of learning as drudgery.

Here's another secret homeschooling parents bring to light. It's okay to agree that some of what "education" forces a child to learn is irrelevant. It beats lying about it, and when you're honest your child is so much more apt to respect your advice that she will go along with what "education" forces her to do anyway. When the air is clear, you're free to encourage more fun, just as homeschooler Linda Jordan of New Hampshire did. After a year and a half of homeschooling, Linda heard her teenaged daughter, Zoe, describe her education philosophy to a relative: "Spend as much time as possible on what you really enjoy and as little time as needed on all the other stuff."

Be patient. Shattering myths is a slow process. Think of how many years and teachers and lectures and tests and homework assignments it took to teach you that learning shouldn't be fun. Be patient. Give yourself and your family plenty of time to get into the groove of the learning lifestyle. Make fun one of your guiding principles, and watch your child soar.

A Desire for Success, Not Fear of Failure

Fear is a powerful motivator. In fact, it's so powerful many people spend their entire lives basing their decisions on it without knowing they're doing so. If you're looking to provide the academic edge to your child, don't allow fear to happen to her. If fear has already become her motivator, it's time to help her develop a new, more positive incentive.

I clearly recall as a child feeling nauseous and insisting to my mother that I not have to go to school that day. I still felt sick the next day. Because there wasn't anything obviously wrong with me, my mother called my teacher for some insight. I was always an excellent student, but that week our class was studying Roman numerals, and they were just flying right over my head. Mom told me about the conversation, helped me figure out the numerals, and I returned to school the next day. It was the first thing I'd run into that I didn't easily comprehend, and fear of failure literally made me ill.

Which child is going to pay more attention, the one who fears he'll lose television privileges if he doesn't get more A's on his next report card or the one who diligently works to better his own performance? Which child will learn more, the one who fears what his classmates will say if he answers (or asks) a question or the one who's confident the answer is Baron von Steuben because he played Revolutionary War "Who Am I?" during dinner last night. Which child is enjoying the journey more, the one who will suffer dad's wrath if she doesn't get into his alma mater or the one who excitedly looks forward to her dream career upon graduation?

The children who pay more attention, learn more, and enjoy their academic journey have a goal of success, not fear. Ergo, they are much more likely to achieve success. Even more important, they are much more likely to consider themselves successful, further ensuring the desired outcome.

MAKE ROOM FOR SUCCESS

Ancient wisdom says, "Only an empty cup can be filled." Making way for a new perspective requires letting go of the old. There are many ways you can help your child do this.

Get It Straight from the Horse's Mouth

The quickest way to discover your child's fears is to talk with her. Children, being children, can harbor fears you couldn't imagine if you spent a month of Sundays trying. Often, it's just a matter of turning a reassuring light on them, just as monsters disappear when it's no longer dark. As my mother discovered, you can eliminate a child's fear by being the loving parent who recognizes the fear and understands it, and then provides a few minutes of guidance to make it go away.

Get the Teacher(s) on the Team

A conference with the teacher, during which you explain how you're working to change your family's educational approach, can greatly help resolve fears. Disclose what your child has told you about her fears enough not to violate her confidentiality and the trust your child placed in you by sharing. (Sad to say, the possibility does exist that the teacher will "spill the beans.")

You'll need your diplomat's hat if your child's fear of failure has its roots in the classroom. Fear of failure grows most quickly in atmospheres of shame, humiliation, or degradation, any or all of which may permeate your child's time at school. If you plunge ahead and point this out to the teacher, the likely result will be a teacher on the defensive, and folks on the defensive tend not to hear what we say.

Instead, focus on the positive. Share your plan for developing the desire for success in your child, along with your enthusiasm. Ask the teacher what she might be able to contribute to the cause. Let her know you're willing to contribute ideas, resources, and maybe even time that she could use to benefit the entire class.

Assess Your Child's Skills

I've lost count of the number of phone calls, letters, and e-mails I receive from parents who recently made a horrific discovery. Despite good grades on report cards, their ten-year-old—or teenager—can't perform simple arithmetic calculations, can't find the United States on a map, or can't read well enough to make sense of a letter from grandma.

You'd better believe a child harboring these kinds of "secrets" operates from a perspective of fear: fear of falling behind, of being thought of as or called stupid, of being found out. Do not assume that good grades on report cards are indications of mastered basics. Assess these skills yourself. You don't need a doctorate in education to figure out how well your child does or does not read, spell, write, or grasp math concepts.

Have your child pick a book for the two of you to read together and take turns. Feign busyness (if you have to) and dictate a note for your child to write to leave for the UPS man (or to fill whatever other need for written matter you may have). Think of skill-appropriate, "real life" math problems to determine your child's ability. ("I'm thinking about serving shrimp at the dinner party this weekend. How many do I need to give each of six guests five shrimp?" "I need to call for estimates on new carpeting tomorrow. Would you measure how many square yards we'll need for the living room?" "I've been thinking about getting a new refrigerator while they're on sale. If the one I want normally costs $649.00, what will it cost with a 15 percent discount, and don't forget to add in the tax so I know the true amount.")

When Jenny Swanson's fourth grade daughter came home from school in St. Charles, Missouri, and Jenny discovered "she had major trouble with reading and spelling, and no learning skills whatsoever," she experimented until she found a method to get her daughter back on track.

"I gave her much smaller assignments that helped her concentrate harder on each," Jenny explains. "We wouldn't move on to anything else until she knew the material. In addition, we did a lot of reading and projects together." Today, Jenny reports, "she enjoys learning more and retains more knowledge."

If you find your child's skills lacking as Jenny did, you, too, can experiment with various approaches and activities until you find what works for your particular child. Knowing his learning style helps narrow down the possibilities and gets you on the road to success quicker.

If you discover your child's skills are at or beyond expected levels, wonderful! If he operates out of fear of failure, it's not because he can't complete what's expected of him.

BUILD CONFIDENCE

I played at a beautiful golf course this summer as part of a foursome of women. All had more experience than I. Two were especially good, and one of these had played this particular course many times. As we rounded a corner about halfway through the game, she said, "Wait until you see this next hole, ladies."

The ladies' tee practically hugs the edge of a ravine at least one hundred yards wide. As everyone groaned, I noted, "It's meant to intimidate you. We've all hit farther than that today. Just play like it isn't even there."

All three teed off before me and all hit various numbers of balls—you guessed it—straight into the ravine. The pressure was on. I kept my eyes on the flag in the distance so I wouldn't see the ravine. I swung, and everyone cheered as the ball sailed over that chasm—right into the edge of the woods on the other side.

All of the other ladies possessed much more skill than I. It was confidence that got my ball across the ravine, confidence built upon success in a previous similar situation so I was not intimidated by the current challenge.

Confidence builds one success at a time until there isn't room for fear. Perhaps your child spends a lot of time in a classroom where the teacher's focus is on failure and looking for what's wrong with a paper, a project, a test, a presentation, not to mention the possibility of peer focus on what's wrong with her hair, clothes, accent, etc.

Create openings for encouragement by giving your student opportunities to succeed. Cultivating the habit of guiding him in following his own interests will help immensely. Also include him in daily activities that provide just enough challenge to be intriguing and that make him stretch, yet that he can accomplish. For example, if you have helped him learn how to determine area when you ordered your new carpeting, let him apply this knowledge in other ways, such as figuring out how much paint you need for the bedroom walls, how much fertilizer for the garden, the optimum size of a dream bedroom, you get the idea. Achievement, encouragement, success, and confidence—what gifts for a child.

At the same time you're emptying your child's cup of fear of failure, start cooking the brew that will take its place, the desire for success.

READY, SET, GOALS!

Read biographies of successful people, or listen to any of America's multitude of self-help gurus, and you get talk about goals—lots of it. You'll learn that it's a lot easier to get there if, first, you know where *there* is and, second, you've figured out the route you plan to take.

Personal goals that come from within are the fastest route to success in academics just as they are with career advancement, buying a new house, or winning your honey's heart. Why, oh why, schools take so much time to teach children about the dangers of drugs instead of goal setting is beyond me. Isn't having a goal a greater deterrent to drug use than learning all the drugs' names and how they can make you feel? A child pursuing goals to make his dreams come true is also less likely to misbehave in class, engage in promiscuous sex, consume alcohol, bully others, or participate in violent and criminal activities. Why? Because goals give him something positive to focus on. Instead of learning being an endless stream of unrelated tasks that stretch on for years, it acquires a purpose. The additional benefit is the child experiences successes all along the way.

Turn Educational Goals and Responsibility Over to Your Child As Soon As Possible

Many folks are shocked to discover the amount of educational autonomy a lot of homeschooled children grow up with. The practice of educational self-direction is based on a sound and simple theory: Children who experience responsibility become responsible, and everything they do reflects this.

While writing a book called *Homeschoolers' Success Stories: 15 Adults and 12 Young People Share the Impact That Homeschooling Has Made on Their Lives* (Prima Publishing, 2000), I interviewed my son, asking about his autonomy. He recalled the first time, at about twelve years of age, that I turned responsibility for the state-required quarterly reports over to him, believing he would better understand what his education was all about by completing them. (Quarterly reports outline the educational activities a child has participated in and roughly coincide timewise with the issuance of report cards in school.)

"I felt very in charge then," he says. "I knew I could get as much accomplished as I wanted. I studied many of the typical high school subjects, often with alternative material. I coordinated what I wanted to study with Mom, set goals, and met those goals, and the rest of the time was available to explore different subjects or do something else I wanted to do."

Another "graduate" of homeschooling in the book is Shannon Cavin, a young lady who serves in the U.S. Navy. "I loved it that I could decide what courses I'd take," Shannon remembers, "and that Mom and I could compare opinions on how well we thought I was doing in my studies. I had control over how much I could learn. There may be people who try to do as little as possible while homeschooling, but why rob yourself when there's so

SIX PRINCIPLES OF SUCCESSFUL LEARNING

- Nurture and exercise curiosity

- Encourage the most effective motivation to learn: intrinsic motivation

- Help make learning fun again

- Develop a desire for success to replace fear of failure

- Study isn't enough; apply your knowledge

- The process of learning is as important as the content

much to learn and you can learn what you want? It's fun, it's exciting, and you can enjoy it so much."

Are you surprised that children in charge of their own education are excited about how much there is to learn and eager about how much they can accomplish? These are not children who are thrilled when there is a snow day or a teacher's workshop that closes the school doors. Might it be those children are happier to stay at home in an environment where they can experience some sense of control over their education, their time, their minds?

As the parent of a traditionally schooled child you can help her assume as much self-direction in her education as possible. Your purpose in doing this is to inspire the same energy, excitement, and passion about learning as your child gets from shouldering other kinds of responsibility.

As always, educational autonomy begins with you talking with your child. You can't expect a six-year-old to decide what college she wants to attend, but you can keep in touch with her about her interests at the moment, what's going on at school, with her friends, with her toys and pets. What is she reading? What would she like to read before bed tonight? What does she think of the new baby next door? If you listen, truly listen, she will tell you everything you need to know. Let her make as many decisions as possible. Request her opinion.

An older child may not at first be familiar enough with the idea of taking responsibility and setting goals. If so, spend some informal time familiarizing him with the concept, then give him permission to speak his mind as you converse about, yes, as corny as it sounds, his hopes, his dreams, his idea of a perfect life. Where does he see himself in five years, ten, twenty? Does he know how to get there, academically or otherwise? Help him find out how. Likely you'll just need to spend enough time getting him started on research (and be sure to explain the research you're doing and how!) before he takes charge.

Above all else, allow the goal to be his: where he wants to go to college, if he doesn't want to go to college, if he thinks he wants to sing in a rap group. Don't worry: It's likely his goal is going to change along the way (didn't yours?). And when he knows how to set and reach a goal, he can apply that knowledge to achieve anything he wants.

Put the goal in writing. Have your child sign it. This is when an idea reinvents itself into commitment.

If you're feeling particularly spunky, you can inform the folks at your child's school about the schools in Maryland, Vermont, Virginia, and Washington, among other states, that have taken the plunge and provide teacher/parent/student-created learning plans for every student. "It's the big buzzword, 'differentiated instruction,'" [a teacher said]. "You don't teach the same thing to everyone. The motto is 'meeting the needs of all learners.'" ("Lessons

Tailored to Fit the Learner, Not Vice Versa," *Seattle Times,* December 10, 2002.)

EVERY JOURNEY BEGINS WITH THE FIRST STEP

Back at that golf course, with an eye on the flag (success), I didn't even see the ravine (failure). No, the ball didn't make it all the way to the flag, but it overcame the greatest obstacle to getting there (I didn't fail right out of the starting gate), and that was the first step.

As soon as your child knows where he wants to go, explain to him that he has to figure out how to get there. Sit in a comfortable place with pencil and paper and jot down ideas. If, in fact, college is the goal and that's eight years away, what steps can he take in that direction in the meantime? Don't forget to include some very short-term goals (these can be weeks for older children, days for younger ones, especially at the beginning, and most especially if your child experiences problems at school). Short-term goals keep the long-term goal fresh and interesting, reachable, and in her thoughts frequently. Each step accomplished builds evermore confidence in your child for the next step. Before you know it, you'll be up all night figuring out how you're going to pay for the university of her choice.

Don't Just Study, Apply!

For a moment, let's assume you changed your mind and want to learn to play golf with me. Certainly we should "hit the books" and learn from the pros who write them. But when we're done reading, should we close the books and think, "Now I know how to play golf"? Or should we grab some clubs and see how our book learning transfers to the driving range?

Most of us have to swing a club more than once to get what the pro means when he advises us to swing "through" the ball, not "at" it. In other words, what we read in those books "sticks" a lot better if we study, then apply our new knowledge. In fact, that's what medical internships and law clerking and probationary job training periods are all about—checking whether or not you can actually do what you have studied.

ADDING APPLICATION TO YOUR CHILD'S LEARNING EXPERIENCE

Some children don't see their schoolwork as relevant to their daily lives because they don't go on to apply what they've learned to real-life situations. Their experience stops with the receipt of the information. They don't get the opportunity to make the information stick. (Remember those cram sessions before exams and how when the test was over some of us were able to forget the material even more swiftly than we were able to "stuff" it into our brains in the first place?) Your child is lucky, though. You can provide the experience of application, bolstered by purpose. (A teacher instructing twenty-five children can't have them all measure the area of the classroom at the same time to follow up on her instruction. She can have them measure as homework, but even that is application without purpose, unless by some quirk of fate all the families are carpeting or painting at the same time.)

Indeed, application of the increasing knowledge your child possesses is a key element of the learning lifestyle. Opportunities abound, especially for reading, writing, and arithmetic, the basics that open up the world to any learner. (We'll talk more about "real world learning" soon in chapter 10.) In the meantime, check a few of your child's current homework worksheets to see what she's supposed to be learning, throw your creativity into high gear, and think of fun ways to get the reading, writing, speaking, spelling, and math lessons woven into the time you're already spending together. For inspiration you might want to get *The Ultimate Book of Homeschooling Ideas: 500+ Fun and Creative Learning Activities for Kids Ages 3–12* (Dobson, Prima Publishing,

2002). This may sound like a shameless plug for the book, but all I did was put it together. Experienced homeschooling parents gladly shared their innovative ideas on helping children learn everything from subtraction to manners, from entomology to public speaking. The collection will keep you busy for years.

NATURE'S PROBLEM-SOLVING PLAYGROUND

Over the years I have received more educational materials for review than most people see in five lifetimes. I'm most perplexed by made-up opportunities for children to learn "problem solving." Isn't the world full of enough real problems that need correcting? Why not start there?

When you help your child apply knowledge, "real problems" always arise. Voila, you've created one of nature's problem-solving playgrounds. Let's use as an example the child who's helping prepare for new carpeting. The area problems in her math textbook always use a perfect rectangle or square. While measuring the living room, she encounters a problem—a closet juts into the perfect rectangle! What to do? Count the space anyway and carpet the closet? Deduct that amount of space? How? Will not deducting the space cost money in wasted carpeting? How much?

This is an opportunity to introduce your child to the concept of choice and consequences. When a child simply takes in information, then proves his intake by answering a multiple-choice test, what are the consequences of getting it wrong? He gets a few points shaved off for his wrong answers, and the final grade isn't what it might have been. Getting it wrong a lot could result in his being held back at the end of the year, but even this is rare today, despite talk to the contrary.

On the other hand, as the example above illustrates, applying knowledge results in real choices. As we've all figured out in our adult lives, real choices have consequences. If a child is fortunate enough to learn this during his teen years, he's more likely to think for himself (offsetting the negative influence of peer pressure), be responsible (better equipped to handle inevitable independence), and focused (desirous of success).

Applying knowledge is a mental exercise worth its weight in gold. Instead of simply receiving information, your child experiences a learning process readily transferable to future problems, in and out of school.

It's the Process That Counts

Have you ever wondered who decides what should be in the curriculum that all children have to learn? Whoever is charged with such an awesome responsibility, shouldn't he/she/they at least tell us why all children should know these things? Wouldn't it be nice if the public—out and about in the world and cognizant of what information they use and don't use—could provide input?

Yeah, I know I'm a dreamer, but considering these questions is more important than ever to parents of children growing up in the Information Age. Now, more than ever, it's crucial to define education for yourself. One reason we educate our children is so they grow into contributing members of society. Let's look at one concept of the Information Age called "just in time." This means there's no need to warehouse products because technology allows orders to be delivered "just in time." There's no need to maintain an office with a conference room when technology can link attendees from the comfort of their homes or offices "just in time." Is it that much of a leap to think that our children, the future contributing members of society, can benefit from just-in-time learning?

With so much information at our fingertips, perhaps it's time to stop narrowing down through a curriculum just what is important for everyone to know. Let's start with the premise that each child is different, developing at her own rate intellectually, emotionally, psychologically, and spiritually. Wouldn't just-in-time learning be as exciting and valuable to her as just-in-time business concepts are to the CEO with an eye on the bottom line?

Applying the just-in-time concept to learning isn't new. Practitioners in information-laden professions do it all the time. Attorneys don't memorize every law; physicians don't learn by heart every symptom of every disease. When they need a particular piece of information, they turn to vast databases of well-organized knowledge. Just-in-time retrieval works for them because they know where to go for information, and they know how to connect it to the task at hand.

LOOK PAST CONTENT AT PROCESS

Herein lies the rub. Equally vast databases of well-organized general and specialized knowledge are now easily available to anyone, not least to our computer-savvy children. Many of those high-achieving homeschoolers you read about have benefited from placing less emphasis on the content of learning (it's everywhere!) in favor of understanding the learning process. Instead of focusing on what to learn, they spend time learning how to learn.

This helps explain why homeschooling parents spend more time thinking about learning than teaching and why teaching credentials aren't necessary to improve your child's school performance. I honestly don't remember what I asked that brought forth the comment, but it stuck with me. One day my now-adult, homeschooled son nonchalantly told me he's much better at "researching" than his friends and peers at work. I asked what he meant. "If there's a problem to solve or something new to do or someone needs information about something, I'm the one who knows how to get things rolling," he explained.

I couldn't help thinking about how my son acquired such a valuable skill. We didn't hold classes on it and I don't remember a single book that addressed the subject. Was it his proximity to someone who was always finding out something new, whether for our homeschooling or my work, volunteerism, or curiosity? Was it because he understood education is achieved, not received, and embraced responsibility for it? Was it because we encouraged him and guided him to follow his interests?

Yes, all of these contributed. They were all part of our learning lifestyle. Many homeschooled children build their academic edge by learning directly from the learning lifestyle itself, and yours will, too.

It's important to note my son and I hadn't previously looked up the exact information, or encountered the same circumstances, for which my son now found his skill useful. Rather, after experimenting with and practicing the process so many times as he grew, he could use it with any learning opportunity, anywhere, any time.

I hope you've noticed how natural the six principles of successful learning are. There are no tricks here; no need for lots of money, resources, or training. The most essential component to making the six principles come alive is you—a loving parent to make sure they remain a priority in your family life.

PART THREE

Focus on: Creating a Favorable Learning Environment

"If you are interested in something, you will focus on it, and if you focus attention on anything, it is likely that you will become interested in it. Many of the things we find interesting are not so by nature, but because we took the trouble of paying attention to them."

MIHALY CSIKSZENTMIHALYI,
*Finding Flow: The Psychology of
Engagement with Everyday Life*

CHAPTER 9

Conditions of Optimal Learning

LINUS PAULING, a poor little boy who grew up to become the recipient of the Nobel prize in chemistry in 1954 and the Nobel peace prize in 1962, wasn't considered a child genius. "What started him on a long and productive life," writes Mihaly Csikszentmihalyi, "was a determination to participate as fully as possible in the life around him."

Many were surprised that Pauling had the curiosity and enthusiasm of a child even when he was ninety years old. "I just went ahead doing what I liked to do," he explained when asked his secret to happiness.

Perhaps there were critics' voices in the background, complaining: "Poor preparation, self-indulgence, total irresponsibility." But, as Professor C. clearly notes, "the point is that Pauling—and the many others who share his attitude—like to do almost everything, no matter how difficult or trivial . . . The only thing they definitely don't like is wasting time. So it is not that their life is objectively better than yours or mine, but that their enthusiasm for it is such that most of what they do ends up providing them with flow experiences." (Flow, as you recall from chapter 2, is the sense of effortless action people feel in moments that stand out as the best in their lives.)

Linus Pauling achieved an academic edge by creating a favorable learning environment for himself. He read the Bible and Darwin's *Origin of Species* before his ninth birthday, collected insects and studied entomology at age eleven, and started a mineral collection at age twelve. At age thirteen, he plunged into chemistry.

Your child has the added benefit of a caring adult, you, to help turn her home and community into an exciting learning environment. What are the conditions of optimal learning that learning guides have discovered? Let's find out.

Enhancing Your Child's Educational Environment

If fifteen years ago I'd have thought to put together a mail-order catalog offering wood and nails to homeschoolers to build their own bookshelves, I'd be rich today. One thing you will never hear a homeschooler say is, "Oh, that's all right; we've got enough bookshelves."

WHY?

An artist's studio has tubes of paint. A carpenter's shop overflows with wood. A learner similarly needs to fill his environment with accessible learning materials. If the computer is dad's for his work and your son may use it only for special projects, it's not accessible. If you keep paints and brushes and clay and stencils on the top shelf in the laundry room, they're not accessible. If you tell your daughter to stay out of the garden, you are denying her access to it. You get the picture.

Certainly your child should have a storage place for his educational materials in his own space. But there's something about

"GOVERNMENTALIZE" FOR HOW CHILDREN LEARN

Here are selected results from a two-year study conducted by the National Research Council for the U.S. Department of Education.

- Young children actively engage in making sense of their world.
  Translation: Little ones are predisposed to learn.

- Young children have abilities to reason with the knowledge they understand.
  Translation: Children are ignorant but not stupid.

- Children are problem solvers and, through curiosity, generate questions and problems; they also seek novel challenges.
  Translation: Children are persistent as learners because success and understanding are motivating in their own right.

- Children develop knowledge of their own learning capacities (metacognition) very early.
  Translation: Children are capable of planning and monitoring their own success and correcting their own errors.

- Children's natural capabilities require assistance for learning.
  Translation: Caring adults can promote children's curiosity and persistence by supporting their learning attempts and keeping the complexity and difficulty of information appropriate for success.

- A lot of "time on task" doesn't ensure learning if it's reading and rereading a text.
  Translation: Busywork doesn't mean learning is happening.

(continues)

"GOVERNMENTALIZE"
FOR HOW CHILDREN LEARN *(continued)*

- Learning with understanding is more likely to promote transfer (of knowledge) than simply memorizing information from a text or a lecture.

  No translation available yet: Because schools still almost exclusively test only students' memories, the researchers still haven't had a lot of experience with the advantages of learning with understanding.

- Knowledge taught in a single context is less subject to transfer than knowledge acquired through a variety of contexts.

  Translation: The process of learning needs to be considered along with content. Children are more likely to hang onto the relevant features or concepts when material is presented in multiple contexts (just as it is in natural contexts). As a bonus, multiple-context presentation also increases understanding of how and when to put knowledge to use (known as conditions of applicability).

- Learning and transfer should not be evaluated by "one-shot" tests of transfer.

  Translation: Typical tests are useless. How well children transfer knowledge, an integral step in learning, can't possibly be perceived until they have an opportunity to learn something new, at which point transfer of old information is evident when they grasp the new information more rapidly. Assessing such evidence of learning is difficult to impossible in a classroom and much easier with your own child.

Adapted from Linda Dobson's The Ultimate Book of Homeschooling Ideas: 500+ Fun and Creative Learning Activities for Kids Ages 3–12 *(Prima Publishing, 2002)* incorporating the materials into all your home's living areas that confirms the message of family-centered learning. It impresses like an open invitation to a friend's home—any day, any time. It entices togetherness, whether you're all doing something in concert or simply side by side.

Your goal is to encourage "extracurricular" learning and a sense of ownership and autonomy when you integrate learning materials into living areas. For best results, encourage your child's input. One of my first published articles, "A Place of Their Own," *(Home Education Magazine,* January/February 1988) tells the story of the epiphany I had one evening after I almost fell asleep creating the next day's "lesson plan." I realized I'd been trying to make homeschool more "fun," instead of making my children's environment a place of their own, "a place tailored to fit the children it serves, not vice versa."

Here's what happened.

Although we kept all the basics, like the globe, maps, pens and pencils, we moved them out of their places of honor and put our personal belongings there instead. Charles wanted our parakeet in the room so we moved the globe. Erika disliked trudging to the attic for the scrap box each time she undertook an art project, so the corner bookcase found a new home in the front room, and the scrap box is now as accessible as her creative ideas.

"What else don't you like about the room, gang?" I asked, eager to please.

"What I'd really like," Erika answered, "is to be able to reach the shelves myself."

So we relocated the shelves lower on the walls, and now, even Adam, the preschooler, can help himself to anything he wants. We gained precious wall space, quickly filled with Charles' favorite planet poster and hanging skeleton model. Erika contributed her recent, painstakingly completed needlepoint project, and suggested we hang a few special photographs from our recent trip to Montreal. Adam returned from the kitchen with a favorite doggy mug to hold pens and pencils on the work table.

Although we were tired and hungry when we finished at noon, we were delighted with the results of our work. After a lunch devoured in record time, all three children hurried back into their room to touch, explore, and independently settle down to paint. Each completed a couple of pages of math, to boot!

WHAT?

Let me stress again that you don't have to mortgage your home to build an interesting, useful collection of educational materials. Some even make great gifts! Of course you will provide a well-lighted table, desk, or cubbyhole. You will need to stock an assortment of paper (lined, unlined, card stock, construction, colored and white copy, handmade, big, small, etc.). When I worked in an office I brought home copious amounts that were going to be thrown away. Writing utensils that encourage practice can include regular and colored pencils; markers and crayons; ballpoint, fountain, calligraphy, and gel pens; a feather pen and berry juice ink for studying the Declaration of Independence; chalk and charcoal; candles and lemon juice for "invisible" writing; etc.

A collection of art supplies inspires creativity: paints (finger, tempera, acrylic, oil), paper and canvas, scissors, glue, tape, string, stamps and ink pad, scrap material, ruler, compass, stencils, clay, Fimo, Legos, beads, yarn, model kits, food coloring, salt dough, carving wood, a collection of rescued "garbage" including empty toilet paper and paper towel rolls, yogurt cups, coffee cans with lids, egg cartons, catalogs and magazines (for cutting out pictures, letters, and numbers), old clothes for dress-up and plays—the list is endless.

How about creating a homemade science kit that includes a magnifying glass, small kitchen scale, binoculars, bug net, funnel, and measuring cups and spoons? Or a collection of math manipulatives: M&M's, pattern blocks, Cuisenaire rods, dice, dominoes, poker chips, dry beans, coins, and buttons?

An older child may appreciate an area where she can work on her hobby, or write, read, or do homework in a comfortable setting of her own design. Keep her learning style in mind as you both determine whether her "space" should be in the middle of the kitchen hubbub or tucked into a quieter part of your home.

No matter the age of your child, if you have a computer, load up on "edutainment" programs that let your child painlessly review school lessons, prepare for a test, and understand basic concepts in greater depth.

Much interesting material is free for the taking from the Internet. Purchase index cards and an inexpensive file box. When you come across a terrific site, jot its name and Web address on the card, along with any helpful notes. (Great math for Susie, Josh will like this when he's a bit older, etc.) You can organize them by child, subject matter, or age appropriateness. You can use a five-star (or dinosaur or soccer ball) system and rate them as to how informative and entertaining each is. Note whether or not the site has materials you can print out and/or so many ideas you just have to revisit it. Of course, let your child also explore the site with you and help you choose materials.

Then there are books, so many books, and magazines, videos, audio books. If finances are tight, scour yard sales and library book sales to help build your home library. Befriend your librarian and make a point of going to the library at least every couple of weeks. This keeps a constant variety of materials flowing through the educational environment as you and your child choose materials based on need, interest, and just for fun.

WHERE?

A bigger challenge than gathering materials in most households is where to put them. You will really get to exercise your creativity muscles as you examine your living quarters for space.

First, look at how you're currently using your space—so many of us waste it. Could you consolidate a couple of junk

CONDITIONS OF OPTIMAL LEARNING

- An environment enhanced with a cornucopia of materials to inspire creativity, awaken curiosity, and build autonomy

- Content of your child's experience explored for its value

- Expanded experience of the world and its offerings

- Maximum "flow" experiences

- Studying a topic of real interest in-depth

drawers? Clear off the old bill pile from the kitchen counter? Get rid of that funky old chair no one ever sits in? Perhaps you can create something out of nothing—a small area at the top of the stairs, a nook or cranny in an older home, a corner of the kitchen, dining, or living room.

Are there places in the attic, basement, garage, mud or laundry rooms? If you live in a mild climate, don't forget your porch, patio, or balcony. Hey, you might even put a roof on the tree fort.

Use shelves, if possible, to help keep resources organized. One homeschooler I know flipped tall narrow bookcases on their sides so her little ones could reach everything. They covered the top with pillows to create a reading area. Some homeschoolers use pegboard to hang some materials and tools. You can also use discarded bulk food containers, plastic sorting bins, cutlery trays, decorated tin cans (watch for sharp edges), and lidded boxes like those used for files storage or that once held ten reams of copy paper. A behind-the-door hanging shoe bag offers a dozen pockets or so to sort and keep materials, or you and your child can make one yourselves. A homeschooling mom sewed pockets from old jeans and other pants onto material and used them as curtains. In the pockets her children store scissors, crayons, and pencils without taking up an inch of precious space. Another mom hangs the letters of the alphabet, with a picture or drawing of an object that begins with that letter, from the ceiling. We used a big, old trunk to store many of our art materials out of sight in the corner, yet easily within the children's reach.

Whatever materials you decide upon and wherever they end up, you'll have to accept that your home will never appear on the cover of *Better Homes & Gardens*. Just remember how much your child will benefit from the resources that are ready at hand when inspiration hits. Living in a well-stocked environment will help her learn to control attention, create educational autonomy, and apply skills she is learning, all vital conditions of optimal learning.

Exploration and Expansion of Experience

"The content of experience will determine the quality of life," writes Professor C. early in his book, *Finding Flow.* This is a simple yet profound statement. Its truth is something we all know deep down inside, and heaven knows we all desire to improve the quality of our lives. Yet how many among us regularly and consciously examine the content of our experience, let alone the experiences of our children?

As a rule, parents living the learning lifestyle try to stay vigilantly aware of the content of their children's experience. No doubt this fuels the fires of "protectionist" criticism that homeschoolers sometimes hear, and in some homes (no one is sure how many or what percentage of overall homeschoolers), the freedom to control content stems from a strongly religious conviction. Still other families have decided that the experiences a growing child can have outside of the school schedule and educational walls are positive and beneficial.

You will be wise to take stock of the experiences that constitute your child's life. Look at both the activities and people that fill her time. Do they help her stretch and grow as a human being? If not, a one-on-one discussion and a reordering of her life aspects may be in order, for no matter how many wonderful ways you may help her, your goals will be negated or overrun if less positive influences prevail. That said, we'll remain focused on the academic aspects of her life.

Professor C. has called the flow experience "a magnet for learning—that is, for developing new levels of challenges and skills. In an ideal situation, a person would be constantly growing while enjoying whatever he or she did." Sure sounds like a condition of optimal learning, doesn't it? Keep your child in mind as we explore the exciting potential of these experiences.

Helping Your Child Explore "Flow"

During over thirty years of trying to answer the question, "What makes a life useful and worth living?" Professor C. has studied humans around the globe. His work is beneficial for parents who see education's purpose as leading children toward a life worth living and not merely toward the best paycheck possible.

Professor C. has already told us in chapter 2 that passive leisure, such as relaxing or watching television, rarely produces flow and that our favorite activities have the best chance of succeeding. (This is why it's so important for a child to receive as much opportunity as possible to pursue interests.) Three main conditions appear to set the stage for the experience of flow:

1. A person faces a clear set of goals that require appropriate responses. Some examples of life activities that make a flow experience include golf (that's why I'm so smitten!), moun-

tain climbing, weaving, playing a musical piece; anything that provides the opportunity to focus on clear and compatible goals.

2. The activity provides immediate feedback. How well one is doing is always extremely obvious: The golfer's ball did or didn't get closer to the hole, the climber slipped or moved higher on the mountain, the last row on the weaver's loom does or doesn't fit the pattern.

3. The challenge is just about manageable, and the person must use his skills to the utmost. The activity is not so easy as to be boring or so difficult as to cause anxiety. When high challenges are matched with high skills, the result is deep involvement.

Implementing some or all of the recommendations in this book is the quickest route to the feeling of flow that enhances your youngster's experience. The best way to ensure your child receives the benefits of the learning that often accompanies flow, then, is to provide her with these conditions as much as possible, every day. Here's Professor C.'s explanation of why it's worth every effort:

> When goals are clear, feedback relevant, and challenges and skills are in balance, attention becomes ordered and fully invested. Because of the total demand on psychic energy, a person in flow is completely focused. There is no space in consciousness for distracting thoughts, irrelevant feelings. Self-consciousness disappears, yet one feels stronger than usual. The sense of time is distorted; hours seem to pass by in minutes. When a person's entire being is stretched in the full functioning of body and mind, whatever one does becomes worth doing for its own sake; living becomes its own justification. In the harmonious focusing of physical and psychic energy, life finally comes into its own.

Children at play, a teen learning chess, a young lady intent on perfecting her jump shot—all could very well be experiencing "flow." (This is why play is so important in children's lives. This is why it's best to leave a curious child alone whenever possible.) Additional methods to increase the possibility of flow experiences include:

- Seeking out congenial surroundings, which are often the source of inspiration and creativity

- Experimenting with surroundings, activities, and companions

- Paying attention to the home environment—clear clutter, redecorate to make your home personally and psychologically comfortable

- Helping your child learn to pay attention to and perhaps keep a diary of how she feels during different activities, times of day, places, and with different companions. Reviewing her information may provide you with many clues for better learning

Expanding Experience

Expanding your child's range of experience may provide the most fun for him. Plan to take advantage of all the educationally stimulating activities your community has to offer. You will quickly learn to do this instinctively as part of your family's learning lifestyle.

Jane Fayette is a single mom with a demanding career in San Francisco. Her two daughters attend the local public school, but when they started acting bored much of the time she decided that no matter what, they would find time for two fun and educational activities each week. "It's much easier to accomplish on weekends," says Jane, "but we'll put our schedules through contortions to be able to make an exciting event or volunteer opportunity. We don't always make it to two a week, but having that as a goal helps keep us aiming high!"

When you visit an art museum, volunteer at the local soup kitchen, or camp out in the woods, you're giving your child much more than an introduction to Monet, a primer on charity, or the chance to decide which of ninety-nine mosquito bites to scratch first. You are building her brain—literally.

Our brains are made up of two kinds of cells: glial cells and nerve cells called neurons with branches called dendrites. Basically, the glial cells nourish the billions of neurons as they busily create and maintain the connections for thinking. The dendrite branches pick up messages from other neurons and send them to the cell's body. From there, the message travels to the axon, the neuron's "out box." After it leaves the out box, the message "jumps" across a gap (synapse) where it is picked up by another neuron's dendrites. This feat happens billions of times each day as we engage in mental activity.

New experiences create new connections, changing the structure of the dendrites and synapses and creating new paths for the messages to travel. A child can learn new skills as the brain becomes more flexible and creates alternative paths to old destinations.

Science is proving that expanded experience is a key to learning. Experience provides children with the "files" of information they need for learning, thinking, reasoning, and making future decisions. "Intelligence enhancement involves creating as many neural linkages as possible," says neurologist Richard Restak in *Mozart's Brain and the Fighter Pilot: Unleashing Your Brain's Potential* (Harmony Publishers, 2002). "But in order to do this, we have to extricate ourselves from the confining and limiting idea that knowledge can be broken down into separate 'disciplines' that bear little relation to one another." (This is why it's so important to integrate learning into your family's daily life without "teaching" or saying, "Okay, now we're baking and learning math; now we're reading and learning phonics.")

There's another reason why exposing your child to a broad range of experience is academically favorable. Have you ever noticed that after you learn something you never knew before, the existence of a new music group, for instance, almost immediately you start hearing the band's name with surprising frequency? That's because "all learning involves transfer from previous experience," say the editors of *How People Learn: Brain, Mind, Experience, and School* (National Academy Press, 1999), the culmination of a two-year study conducted by the National Research Council at the request of the U.S. Department of Education. Because there is no guarantee any child will transfer previous knowledge to a new learning task, the researchers recommend that teachers identify the "learning strengths" that a child possesses, and build on them. (It's important for you to identify your child's learning strengths and preferred styles so you can help your child capitalize on his potential at home.)

So get out, meet the neighbors, see the world, have fun optimizing learning!

Learn One Thing In-Depth

What is your child interested in—Legos, dinosaurs, fashion, cars, video games, electric guitar? It's hard to imagine a child studying any of these topics as a condition of optimal learning, but then children are always full of surprises, aren't they?

The key here is not the topic of in-depth study, but the act of in-depth study itself. As we've already discovered, it's a lot more fun to study something we're interested in, whatever that may be. Here's Professor C.'s take on the topic:

To pursue mental operations to any depth, a person has to learn to concentrate attention. Unless we learn to concentrate, and are able to make an effort, our thoughts will scatter and we will fail to reach any conclusion.

Concentration requires more effort when it goes against the grain of emotions and motivations. A student who hates math will have a hard time focusing attention on a calculus textbook long enough to absorb the information it contains, and it will take strong incentives (such as wanting to pass the course) for him to do so. Usually the more difficult a mental task, the harder it is to concentrate on it. But when a person likes what he does and is motivated to do it, focusing the mind becomes effortless even when the objective difficulties are great.

As in Professor C's example, most children receive plenty of opportunity in school to try to build essential attention and concentration skills in subjects they're not necessarily interested in. By encouraging a form of freely chosen study during nonschool time, you give your child an optimal chance to focus, attend, and concentrate and, thus, to learn. After all, no matter how naturally talented, one doesn't become a good pianist or chemist or politician or doctor or auto mechanic without having invested a lot of attention in learning what is necessary.

Once your child learns to focus, attend, and concentrate on in-depth study, he has gained the ability to transfer these important study skills to subjects that may be less appealing but are necessary nevertheless. "All learning involves transfer from previous experience." This is the same idea as teaching a man how to fish instead of providing him with a fish to eat each day. In our case, you're helping your child learn how to learn. You are helping to feed his mind for a lifetime.

So let the subject be whatever your child decides—success stories abound! A young girl allowed to bring home roadkill for study grows up to become a biologist. A little boy who loved boats climbs the ranks in the Coast Guard. A young man who enjoyed the business side of his paper delivery route becomes a multimillionaire entrepreneur. Having received enough evidence after a few years, one mom trusted and didn't interrupt her son's seeming obsession with viewing old television sitcoms and cartoons. In his teen years he advanced to study the psychology of humor. Today, as an aspiring writer, his college teachers rave about his use of humor. About seven years ago my own household shook with the discordant sounds of a beginning bass guitar player accompanying blaring songs I wouldn't have chosen for anything less than golf with Mel Gibson. My requests for a Beatles song or two went unfilled. But my son had learned how to learn, and through the years that bassist also taught himself how to play guitar and keyboard, becoming quite talented on all of them.

I hope these stories illustrate that while the topic of interest was not one the parents liked or even encouraged, they had no way of foretelling where that innate interest, well studied, would lead. This adds to the wonder and excitement of it all. I've yet to hear one parent say she was sorry she allowed this freedom, or that the results were negative. I believe, as Professor Csikszentmihalyi says in *Finding Flow*, this is why:

> In principle any skill or discipline one can master on one's own will serve: meditation and prayer if one is so inclined; exercise, aerobics, martial arts for those who prefer concentrating on physical skills. Any specialization or expertise that one finds enjoyable and where one can improve one's knowledge over time. The important thing, however, is the attitude towards these disciplines. If one prays in order to be holy or exercises to develop strong pectoral muscles, or learns to be knowledgeable, then a great deal of the benefit is lost. The important thing is to enjoy the activity for its own sake and to know that what matters is not the result but the control one is acquiring over one's attention.

After discovering the pleasure and effectiveness of such learning and not wanting to be left in their children's dust, many

THE ANIMAL SCHOOL

Once upon a time, the animals decided they must do something heroic to meet the problems of a "New World," so they organized a school. They adopted an activity curriculum consisting of running, climbing, swimming, and flying. To make it easier to administer, all animals took all subjects.

The duck was excellent in swimming, better in fact than his instructor, and made excellent grades in flying, but he was very poor in running. Since he was low in running he had to stay after school and also drop swimming to practice running. This was kept up until his webbed feet were badly worn, and he was only average in swimming. But average was acceptable in school, so nobody worried about that except the duck.

The rabbit started at the top of the class in running but had a nervous breakdown because of so much makeup in swimming.

The squirrel was excellent in climbing until he developed frustrations in the flying class where his teacher made him start from the ground up instead of from the treetop down. He also developed charley horses from overexertion, and he got a C in climbing and a D in running.

The eagle was a problem child and had to be disciplined severely. In climbing class he beat all the others to the top of the tree but insisted on using his own way of getting there.

At the end of the year, an abnormal eel that could swim exceedingly well and could also run, climb, and fly a little had the highest average and was valedictorian.

The prairie dogs stayed out of school and fought the tax levy, because the administration would not add digging and burrowing to the curriculum. They apprenticed their children to the badger and later joined the groundhogs and gophers to start a successful private school.

R. H. Reeves, Educator

homeschooling parents go on to apply the principle to their own lives. Yours truly unearthed a passion for writing only when I began homeschooling my children and saw the wonderful proof of the power of focus and concentration growing right under my nose.

CHAPTER 10

Out and About: It's Only Natural

ONCE UPON A TIME, researchers interested in learning performed an experiment with rats. Two groups of rats received the same amount of food and water, but some lived in "impoverished" cages while others enjoyed an "enriched" environment—bigger cages, more friends, and lots of toys to keep them busy and curious.

The rats living in the impoverished cages weighed more than the "rich" rats, but their brains were inferior in two aspects significant to learning. "First," explains Dr. Jane Healy in her report on the research in *Endangered Minds: Why Children Don't Think and What We Can Do About It* (Touchstone, 1990), "there are many more glial support cells in the enriched brains, and second, the neurons themselves have more dendrite spines and thus, presumably, more synapses." (You'll remember from the previous chapter that glial cells nourish the all-important neurons that create and maintain connections for thinking. Dendrite spines deliver messages to neurons before the messages "jump" across gaps to be picked up by another neuron's dendrites.) In addition, the enriched rats "appear to pick up more and different information during exploration as a result of their lively curiosity."

It gets more interesting. Researchers were also keeping an eye on a group of control rats that grew up "in the wild" outside the lab. These rats were exposed "to the real challenges of living in a free environment," explains Dr. Healy, "finding food, defending themselves, and moving about when and where they wish." For the purpose of our discussion, let's consider these rats as closer to "living the learning lifestyle."

The researchers found that as beneficial as it is, the "enriched" environment didn't stimulate the rats' brains as well as the natural one, where the rats "tend to have larger and heavier cortexes than do those raised in cages." Cortexes, Dr. Healy explains in her book, are "the control panels for processing information at three levels: receiving sensory stimuli, organizing them into meaningful patterns so that we can make sense out of our world, and associating patterns to develop abstract types of learning and thinking." While rat research doesn't translate directly to humans, it has some clear implications: Being "out and about" is not only natural, it is good exercise that builds highly-functioning brains.

Homeschooling families don't necessarily know of this research. They have discovered the benefits of integrating children into the workings of the greater world by, well, integrating children into the workings of the greater world. Like you, homeschooling parents need to accomplish daily chores, and whether that means going to the grocery store or the state capital, to the dentist or the attorney's office, they make sure their children accompany them.

Where Did Adults Learn the Things They Know and Use?

As a veteran of the education process, you have a track record to look back on, so let's look. Think about your thirteen years of required school attendance. (Take your time: I'm not going anywhere.)

First, and be honest now, how much do you remember from those days about things like the Battle of Hastings, trigonometry, the inner workings of an earthworm? Would you be able to pass today the same tests you passed in high school? Second, beyond the biology classroom, how often have you applied your knowledge about earthworm entrails, or any other subject covered in school, as you go about daily life?

Next, think about the information you *do* use in your normal routines. Where did you learn how to balance your checkbook, change a diaper, fit as many dishes as possible into the dishwasher, change a tire? Where did you learn how to move that real estate, inspire the slowest child in your class, create beautiful quilts, be an effective board or council member?

Likely, you picked up these skills and countless others outside of the schoolhouse, either apprenticing with a parent or other adult or out of the need to take care of yourself and your family. (If you learned the basics of your job at college or trade school, remember that this was voluntary study beyond your required school days.)

"The most useful and important learning tools are rarely found within the realm of 'curricula,'" says veteran homeschooler Lillian Jones. "Just as adults find their most important learning in the real world and the most unexpected and natural situations, it's the same for children."

Being out and about doesn't just build brain muscles. It also opens up a world of learning opportunities in the same forum most adults find effective—real life.

So Who Do You Hang Out With?

Let's look at one more interesting aspect of your life—the people with whom you work and choose to spend time. In thinking about these folks, what do you find? Likely some of them are older and others younger than you. Some live nearby and others in different cities and towns.

So what would you think if, upon arriving at work tomorrow, all of the twenty-one-year-olds were herded into one department and all of the fifty-year-olds into another? What if they were then further subdivided depending on what city or town they live in? Wouldn't your work life grow a little more boring if you could only work with those who are the same age and from the same neighborhood as you are?

Never in the real world is the age and neighborhood separation of the school environment repeated, and for good reason. We learn a lot from older, experienced coworkers and get inspired by the energy and enthusiasm of the younger ones. We hold interests and skills in common across age barriers, and we keep up with our professions and hobbies by sharing time and information with folks who may not be exactly like us. If fortunate enough to be in a position to hire our coworkers, the criteria we use for selection will be much more relevant to success than their ages and zip codes.

Just think of the amount of time your child spends with her same-age peers from the same neighborhood, and you will see how narrow is her social sphere. Pay particular attention to the number of adults in your child's life. Learning guides find that adult relationships are priceless for children's lives, because adults have experience and perspectives that children don't receive from their peers.

"My daughter has loved drawing and art since the day she could hold a crayon in her little fist," explains Ohio's Carol Narigon. "I mentioned her interest to a couple of professional artists I know, and both have encouraged her. One gently critiques her work, offers suggestions, and shows her how he gets certain effects with pastels. The other invites her over to play with paints and canvas."

Being out and about also provided unexpected opportunity for Carol's son, a budding musician. "A mom in our homeschool group asked if my son would be interested in helping a popular local musician set up his huge rhythm sculpture display at a day-

PLACES TO VISIT IN YOUR COMMUNITY

Social Studies/Business

Post Office	Newspaper office and printing facility
Airport	Bank
Professional offices	Florist
Publisher	Bakery
Train station	Music and ethnic festivals

Restaurant that serves meals from the country your child is studying

Public Safety/Civics

Firehouse	Hospital
Police Station	City hall/courthouse
State capitol building	Town or city board meeting/public hearing

Science

Farms of all types	Factories of all types
Ranches	Research centers
Fish hatchery	State forest preserve
Hospital	Veterinarian's office
Planetarium/aquarium/zoo	

History

Historical homes and homesteads

Old cemeteries, forts, mines, battlefields

Historical sites-turned-museums

long festival for handicapped children," says Carol. "At this point he's done it for two years, staying all day to help kids play and show them how drumming works. Since then," she adds, "the musician has asked my son to set up and play with his group at a downtown event—for pay."

The rewards of including adults in a child's social circle transcend art critiques and paychecks, though. "These and other adults are important in my children's lives and will help shape the interests and passions that will define their being." Carol adds, "Don't be afraid to tell people about your children's interests, and encourage your children to do the same. People who are actually doing the work often have more to offer than teachers who are following state guidelines."

Your child's relationships with younger children are also valuable. Spending time with little people increases your child's patience, builds empathy, and gives your child a great excuse to be silly for a while. Oftentimes, the older child finds himself the role model instead of a student, a welcome change that often increases self-confidence and esteem.

The Community As Classroom

Why are homeschoolers always out and about? Because they think of their communities as giant classrooms ripe for exploration and replete with learning experiences with people who apply their knowledge every day. All the money in the world couldn't build or buy your child a more vital and useful learning laboratory than the one that already exists around the corner.

CONTEXT: GIVING LEARNING SOMETHING TO HANG ON

Is your child talking about becoming an architect? Has she wondered out loud what the bank does with all that money? Has she asked you why you complain about having to fill out an income tax return every year? Does she seem more interested in the scenery than the play? Regardless of her specific curiosities, here are opportunities to provide context for the reading, writing, and arithmetic skills she's been studying. She can:

- Write to the architect and ask to see and talk about the work he does all day (writing/business communication)

- Read a book from the library and information on the Internet about the workings of banks (reading)

- Help you perform the calculations for your income tax return (arithmetic)

- Call the set designer prior to attending the next performance and ask for a backstage look-see before or after the play (oral communication skills).

Context, say learning lifestylers, is an exceptional motivator. Even the most resistant speller, for example, will want her letter to the architect to be the best it can be. Unenthusiastic readers change their tune when they want to know about something specific. (Homeschooling pioneer Grant Colfax, who appeared on the *Johnny Carson Show* upon acceptance to Harvard where he trained to become a doctor, didn't learn to read until after he was ten when he wanted to know more about the Indian artifacts he kept finding on the family's goat farm.) Some youngsters will think it's pretty cool to be included on something as important as the family's income tax return. And many an introverted child peeks out of her shell for something as exciting as a backstage pass.

If your child is reluctant to meet strangers, let her see you set up the first activity or two as you model appropriate behavior for her. Don't be afraid to ask people for a brief tour or other introduction to their work. Most are more than happy to speak with a child or family interested enough to ask. (Wouldn't you be?)

Success builds upon success, and this approach to learning gets easier with each step as your child's confidence and knowledge base grows with each experience.

VISITING MUSEUMS

Homeschoolers visit museums a lot, and they're not the kids running around with clipboards, frantically trying to find the answers to a list of questions. They rarely take audio tours that have them blindly following a voice that directs them to the "most important" paintings or objects, telling them what to see. Rarely are they the ones following a docent around. They are the ones exploring excitedly for an hour or two, focusing on what interests them.

All sorts of museums are storehouses of information and artifacts that are best explored at leisure in small doses. What sparks an interest one day might leave a person cold on another. Children usually gravitate to what interests them at the moment, and of course this often means the flashiest exhibit with the most buttons. Why not? I want my children to feel that museums are wonderful fascinating places where every visit brings new insights. And so we go a lot, and we purchase memberships to as many different museums as we possibly can, so that short trips don't seem wasteful. I let the children lead the way and don't insist on their reading every explanation as they go. I read what interests me and so do they. We talk, we try, we play. I insist on good etiquette: low voices, no running, and proper use of interactive equipment. Otherwise we are all free to explore.

Over time, I've been amazed at how much they've learned, especially when I haven't actually seen them carefully studying the information presented. Time and again they've demonstrated weeks later that something they saw or experienced at a science or natural history museum has "clicked" and they "get it." They've grown to love certain paintings at the art museum and have wanted to read more about favorite artists or periods or even try a technique at home. Mostly I've been amazed to witness, though not really understand, the process by which they gradually build their own knowledge and understanding of the world by integrating what they know from other sources with information and experiences they've picked up from museums. At ages eleven and thirteen they've even become critics, finding errors in explanations and coming up with suggestions for improvement in exhibit design and presentation.

I don't think any of this would have happened if they'd had to spend long hours in single (or rare) visits and been forced to stop and read everything along the way, if they'd been required to try and get it all, ready or not. Being free to explore means they can absorb and assimilate information for themselves when the time is right for them. They can take time and figure things out for themselves. Even when it seems they're "just fooling around," later discussions reveal how much their minds were actively engaged. It's not necessary to answer someone else's questions or to have the experience in any way predigested and packaged for them. It's actually harder when one has to make one's own connections and draw conclusions. *That's* real learning that endures and opens up avenues for further study and contemplation.

Paula Russell
Sammamish, WA

THE COMMUNITY, LIFE'S BUFFET FOR THE MIND

We wouldn't dream of feeding our children the same food day after day. Everyone knows that physical health depends on ingesting a wide variety of foods because each contributes something unique to overall health. In addition, children would likely hide when called to dinner if they knew meat loaf awaited them for the tenth evening in a row—how boring is that?

Children receive equal benefits from an assortment of "foods for the mind" that contribute to their mental health and give them the excitement of trying something new. I see my local

TOWARD A HAPPY FIELD TRIP

While making arrangements for your trip, ask your host if there's anything you can discuss with your child, including vocabulary, to prepare for the visit. Places that see a lot of school groups often provide information sheets beforehand. Exchange information on what your guide will explain and what you'd like your child to learn. Ask how many visitors can be accommodated; maybe you'd like to invite another family or your learning group.

If you'll have young ones in tow, schedule your trip for a time they're at their best, well fed and well rested, so you, too, can enjoy yourself. Join your children in asking questions, bring paper and pencils for notes, and don't forget the camera!

Talk about your trip on the ride home. Share your ideas about what you found most interesting, things you learned that you didn't know before, and what your visit inspired you to learn next. This encourages your child to examine the trip, increasing its educational value.

Don't forget to send your field-trip host a thank you note. Encourage your child to include comments about what she liked best and what she learned.

Adapted from Linda Dobson's Homeschooling:
The Early Years: Your Complete Guide to Successfully Homeschooling
the 3- to 8-Year-Old Child *(Prima Publishing, 1999)*

community as a "mind buffet," a collection of interesting, colorful, healthy choices that make me hungry just to consider them. (Yes, there are probably a few less savory dishes as well.) As at a buffet, there is so much to pick from that your child doesn't/couldn't possibly take everything. She can leave behind the lima beans, and instead, take an extra large helping of the macaroni salad she likes. Choices are available to all who partake of the feast, as are reviews of the food for prospective diners who want to know what it tastes like. Let's explore some ways to increase your child's appetite for learning, shall we?

LEARNING COOPERATIVES AND GROUPS

Necessity is the mother of invention! We should be glad that homeschooling families felt the need for informal/formal get-to-gethers/classes based on the hobbies/subjects/books/play that interested their children. While the group-learning idea has caught the attention of many marketers who have a program to sell, there are still many groups conceived and organized by moms and dads strictly to help their children. You and/or your child can form a group or cooperative, too, anywhere, anytime.

"My daughters can't *wait* for Thursday nights," says divorced mom Rita Bowers. On Thursdays the girls rush home from their suburban Atlanta school to prepare for "American Girls Night," a "group of nine families with children ranging in age from six to twelve, about half of whom are homeschooled," says Rita. "We meet in a local church, and the only requirement is an interest in the American Girls books, upon which all the activities are based."

The concept is simple: Create an opportunity to get together with others with similar interests to fill your child's need or desire to learn more. Each group is unique because of the needs and personalities of those involved, and they run the gamut from relaxed get-togethers to traditional classes; from short to long term; from daily to monthly; from an hour to an entire day. They can be expensive or purposefully low-cost so the greatest number of families can participate. (Many venues also offer greatly reduced rates to groups.) It's interesting that learning cooperatives and groups are often based on the interests and not the ages of the participants.

Cooperatives incorporate a twist. As the name implies, many families cooperate so as to offer a broader array of possibilities. For example, one parent may give classes on Mondays in creative writing. On Tuesdays, someone else explores the connection between history and mathematics. The group may decide to make every first Thursday field-trip day and Friday evenings a potluck get-together.

Some groups hire teachers, splitting the cost between attendees. These classes cost each family a lot less than a private tutor, keep the ratio of learners to teacher to a low that public schools would envy, and can be readily tailored by the teacher as the children's needs change.

If your child is struggling with a subject, he may show success in a learning group or cooperative. This different approach to the material and alternative approach to learning may be just what he needs. At the other end may be a child who is way ahead of the crowd in a subject or field at school. She can attend a group to build upon knowledge she already has.

Your child's learning preferences should guide you in designing these group gatherings. Your child may be a kinesthetic learner who'd rather hop around than sit still at a desk and/or need to *do* to learn, or she may possess a quiet nature or tend to be introverted and so prefer smaller crowds, or he may be a right-brained artist who thinks left-brainers are all from Mars.

If you don't get it completely right the first time, try again. Experiment with the schedule, the material, the method of presentation, the mix and number of attendees, location, time of day, you name it.

Finding other traditionally schooled children to join your child isn't as hard as you might at first think. It's simply a matter of getting the word out far and wide, while remaining patient. This is no time to be shy. Tell everyone at work, at the doctor's office, in the line at the grocery store. These people may know someone who might be interested in joining or is knowledgeable on the topic and would happily talk with the group or can recommend a great book, Web site, television program, or article they just discovered. Let school personnel know about it, too.

WHERE TO FIND INTERESTING PEOPLE IN YOUR NEIGHBORHOOD

- Local or regional arts council: craftspeople, artists, actors, musicians

- Library or bookstore: writers, poets, craftspeople

- State agricultural extension office: farmers, foresters, nursery and fishery workers

- Chamber of Commerce: business, professional, or service people

- Civic, municipal, and government bodies: legislators, judges, police officers, firefighters, town clerk

Make a nice flyer and hang it around town on the coffee shop, diner, health food store, bank, and laundromat bulletin boards. Think about places where families spend time. If you'd like to find homeschoolers, also tack up notices at the library, ice and roller skating rinks, park entrances, and bowling alleys. What the heck—try the local golf course clubhouse, too. Place an ad in the local paper or in a give-away parenting or money-saver paper.

ONE-FAMILY "GROUPS"

If it suits your family better, you don't need a big group to enjoy educational adventures. Some folks prefer to attend activities as a family instead of with others. Other folks who live in remote areas may find it takes time to build up a group, and, in the meantime, there are places to go and people to meet. In addition, your family's free time may not occur at typical times. Sometimes, younger children are better able to focus without a group to distract them. Going places as a family also makes you more flexible in case something comes up or someone gets sick. Some families are large enough to be their own group!

A small, family-sized group has advantages. A business proprietor may be more comfortable meeting with a few instead of a crowd. In limited physical spaces the family group may be the only option. You may also have the opportunity to actually use equipment or tools, because everyone can get a turn.

I once arranged a tour for my three children and me at the local regional airport. An experienced pilot acted as guide and showed us every nook and cranny of the airport (this was way before September 11) and answered all of our questions. When we returned to our starting place and I thought we were done, he asked if we had a little more time—he wanted to take us for a ride in his plane! He flew over our house and other familiar landmarks. The children were ecstatic! My eldest sat up front and actually flew the plane for a hair-raising minute or so. The youngest turned green but miraculously didn't throw up. Had we arrived at the airport with a dozen other children and several more parents, we wouldn't have had this wonderful adventure. My children still remember it with smiles.

APPRENTICESHIPS

Once upon a time, a young teen named Benjamin Franklin learned to be a printer at his brother's business. For centuries, and even today in some European countries, teens make the transition into the work world by serving as apprentices in an established workplace.

If your child wants to know more about a skill, be it artistic, life enhancing, or future-job-related, he may find an apprenticeship is a rewarding approach. Some artisans and business owners are happy to just pass on their skills to a child, but it's much fairer when there is reciprocal benefit and the child does something in exchange for the training he receives. Your child can baby-sit once a week in exchange for apprenticing with a bookkeeper. She can learn from the gardener down the street in exchange for mowing and trimming the senior gardener's lawn. She could cook a couple of meals a week for the busy veterinarian who can offer hands-on experience in every aspect of his business, from marketing to dealing with grief-stricken pet owners. One of my sons began by dusting and sweeping a small rock shop in exchange for learning lapidary skills.

You should definitely be involved in setting up apprenticeship and mentoring relationships to ensure there is a meeting of the minds between the expectations you and your child have and the expectations of the cooperating adult. You also want to be completely sure your child isn't exploited or exposed to *any* danger—make sure the other adult knows you're always there, looking out for your child's best interests. Speak up and ask for what you want, keeping in mind that some folks will need a bit more information to understand the idea, want to meet with you and your child first, and could possibly say sorry, no. Neither you nor your child should take this personally nor let it stop you from continuing your search for a beneficial apprenticeship.

Start slowly. Sometimes a great match that looks good in the beginning does not work out. Agree on hours per day, days per week, and an overall deadline (one month, six weeks, etc.) at which time both parties may decide if they want to continue or fine-tune the agreement. Finally, prepare a written agreement outlining your understanding, and you, your child, and the other adult sign it.

Find a Mentor

My dictionary defines a mentor as "a wise and trusted counselor or teacher." Imagine the learning that goes on when a child finds a great mentor! Homeschooled children learn with mentors all the time, either in person or by taking advantage of computer communication, and yours can, too.

All three of Cynthia Reynolds' children found mentors in different areas in different ways. "My elder daughter sent a heartfelt fan letter to a favorite author and that started a relationship where she sends her writing to the author who then offers suggestions and constructive criticism," Cynthia explains. "My son participated in a Scout Explorer program, and a dedicated fireman took him under his wing. A naturalist, impressed with my youngest's enthusiasm for the nature center, currently devotes extra time so she can soon lead group tours."

While apprenticeships are typically arranged affairs, mentorships more often blossom slowly, usually as a result of a successful apprenticeship. Professionals are busy people, but at the same time they recognize promise, enthusiasm, and responsibility in a teen and may be very happy to lend a hand in the child's growth. Stories abound of homeschooled children creating their own first jobs this way! The opportunity to function in a responsibility-filled capacity has given many teens the knowledge, skills, and personal relationships that employers value.

Volunteering, Giving Back to the Community

Lest we forget, learning lifestyle families don't just take from the community. They know that giving something in return is equally as vital to their children's education. If necessary, as with younger children, or if possible with any aged child, consider volunteering *with* him. In this way you'll know firsthand what he is experiencing so you may share thoughts, ideas, impressions, and learning with each other.

If you've never checked out your community for volunteer opportunities, you're in for a treat of endless choices. Some families like to volunteer in libraries, museums, nature centers, political campaigns, and all places educational where children can't help but pick up knowledge. On the altruistic side, other families

WAYS TO USE THE COMMUNITY TO INCREASE YOUR CHILD'S ACADEMIC SUCCESS

- Learning groups and cooperatives can address all learning interests and needs and are flexible enough to support the format that best fits your family's lifestyle.

- Apprenticeships are back in style and provide teens with real life, hands-on experience in the work world.

- Trusted mentors provide priceless counseling and can become impressive role models to students.

- Giving back to the community by volunteering is a learning experience that transcends subject matter.

- Informally taking advantage of your community's learning opportunities is fun and rewarding, and it strengthens family bonds.

choose soup kitchens, animal shelters, nursing and convalescent homes, hospitals, Meals on Wheels, Habitat for Humanity, literacy organizations, or completing household chores for elderly or infirm neighbors.

You can help your child get the ball rolling. Use your contacts, or friends' contacts, to find out what opportunities exist. Discuss with your child the pros and cons of any particular choice, listening well to her comments. The most successful experiences involve a good match between the interests of the organization and the interests of your child.

While volunteering is a way to give something back to the community, it is also a way for your child to learn at the same time. Often this type of learning transcends mere subject matter. Every experience offers rewards, be they knowledge about a profession, new adult friendships and possible apprenticeships, empathy, compassion, respect, or a very real sense of belonging that your child may not otherwise feel. These feelings all inspire that important intrinsic motivation to do well in studies.

Out and About As a Family

Many of the most memorable learning experiences result from informally heading out as a family into the neighborhood on a beautiful Saturday afternoon with no particular place to go. I like to think of these excursions as leaving behind the professional educational-tour planner with his strict itinerary and schedule and instead just stopping at inviting places along the way. You're sure to choose places of interest to family members, because . . . why not?

The mind buffet of community is virtually an endless feast for your student. Make a family pact to visit at least once a month a neighborhood spot you've never seen before. Give your child a taste of what awaits, and he'll soon find himself enjoying healthy, wholesome learning experiences.

PART FOUR

Focus on:
Your Important Role

"The young leading the young is like the blind leading the blind; they will both fall into the ditch. The only sure guide is he who has often gone the road which you want to go. Let me be that guide, who have gone all roads, and who can consequently point out to you the best."

THE EARL OF CHESTERFIELD,
letter to his son, 1700s

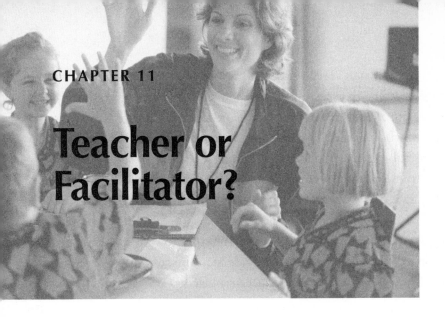

CHAPTER 11

Teacher or Facilitator?

MARIA VON TRAPP so believed in the value of play that she turned her bedroom drapes into material for children's play clothes.

A blind, deaf, and dumb girl overcame all three disabilities with devoted attention from her teacher, Ann Sullivan.

In the land of make-believe, child caretaker Mary Poppins could even make medicine taste good.

We're inspired by the sheer power of love and devotion when we hear these stories. Perhaps we even spend a few moments wondering why life can't be this wonderfully happy and successful for every child on earth. Then we quietly return to the imperfect life we live every day. Maria Von Trapp, the handicapped girl's teacher, and Mary Poppins must have been stronger, smarter, more patient than we are. Likely the children with whom they worked were exceptional from the start. Things were different back then.

Guess what? These women were not stronger, smarter, or more patient than the rest of us; the children weren't necessarily exceptional from the start (when we take one road, we will never know what would have happened on the other); and children were still children back then. The difference, I'm convinced, is that these women respected and understood children, and when they saw that spark of genius in each of them they acted as their facilitators instead of teachers. As I keep reminding you, you don't need to be a teacher to help your child toward academic excellence. It's your respect and understanding of your child that qualify you to serve as a very successful facilitator.

Just So We're Clear

I was afraid of this. Published in 1973, my dictionary doesn't list a definition for facilitator. It's one of those modern day verbs-turned-nouns, like parent(ing) and homeschool(ing). The verb form, facilitate, means "to free from difficulties or obstacles; make easier; aid; assist." This, in a nutshell, is the work of a facilitator.

To compare apples with apples, the verb "teach" is defined in the same dictionary as "to impart knowledge or skill to; give instruction to."

Countless homeschooling parents "teach," many with good academic results. An equal number of homeschooling parents figure if their children are skipping traditional schooling, they can skip traditional teaching, too, with impressive academic results. This is not to say that if a homeschooled child asks mom to teach him how to add she would deny him. Homeschooling parents have learned that a child asking for instruction is truly interested, and an interested child soaks up skills painlessly in comparison to a bored and uninterested child. In this way mom has freed the child from an obstacle to learning—lack of interest. In addition, many moms have discovered their children are much more amenable to obtaining knowledge through real-life scenarios than by literally being instructed.

Finding Your Comfort Zone in Your Child's Education

Of course, the decision how best to go about helping your child achieve her academic goals is yours. You're the one who knows her best, and you know yourself best, too. If your child thrives in a school setting, and you're both comfortable and successful with you performing like a traditional classroom teacher, proceed full speed ahead. My greater concern is the multitude of parents who shy away from helping their children because they have designated this task to teachers, on the theory that they are specialists who have spent years in college and know much more about the way to instruct. On the slim chance you haven't gotten the idea by now, let me say it: *There is no one right way to learn.* If there is no one right way to learn, there is no one right way to instruct!

This opens up a wide arena for you to find your comfort zone in your child's educational process. I'm a proponent of the facilitator approach for four main reasons. One, it's easier for everyone. Two, it tends to keep learning more interesting, rewarding, exciting, and fun. Three, it contributes to a lifelong appreciation of learning. Four, I've tried it in my own home and informally researched results with hundreds, if not thousands, of other families. It really works. Let's find out why, and how you can do it, too.

The Difference Between a Teacher and a Facilitator

Recall that the idea of facilitating turns attention toward the one being helped, whereas teaching, to impart knowledge or give instruction to, shines a spotlight on the helper. With the facilitator, the goal is to clear the path for an active learner. With the teacher, the goal is for the learner to remain comparatively passive while the active participant is the teacher who doles out knowledge, doing something *for* or *to* the student. The implications of these differences are astounding.

For your student it means taking increased responsibility for, and therefore ownership, of his education. Granted, you can't change this perspective within the school, but even a dose of such ownership in your home will have your child taking leaps not baby steps toward those goals of maturity, responsibility, and self-reliance. Incidentally, these are some of the qualities that have college and university admissions officers actively recruiting homeschooled students. Look at this excerpt from a January/February 2002 article in *Brown Alumni Magazine*. "These kids are the epitome of Brown [University] students," says Joyce Reed, who became an associate dean of the college twelve years ago. "They've learned to be self-directed, they take risks, they face challenges with total fervor, and they don't back off."

At age seventeen, Samantha Bouyea's older son applied to four universities and was accepted at all of them. "When the fourth acceptance letter arrived," Samantha remembers, "he credited my 'I'm here to help' facilitator approach to his education. He said he didn't know how things would have turned out had we done it differently, but he's happy not to know!"

Facilitating in lieu of teaching also means that your child isn't going to receive more of what she got all day in school when she returns home. Can you imagine coming home after work only to race through dinner so you can give a lecture on solids, liquids, and gases, or tackle an *extra* page of algebra problems? Can you imagine your child waiting in anxious anticipation? I didn't think so.

The many parents turned off by the notion of becoming their children's teachers can think in terms of facilitating, instead. It's easier, more rewarding, much more likely to be graciously accepted

NATIONAL SPELLING BEE WINNER FAMILY

In 2000, Alison Miller was one of three homeschoolers who finished first, second, and third in the Scripps Howard National Spelling Bee. Her sister Catherine was a fellow contender. Their mom, Mary O'Keefe, describes her family's philosophy as "knowledge is a wonderful thing—the more you give away, the more you have for yourself because you deepen your own understanding in the process." Now Mary shares another homeschooling secret. Here's the "homeschooling twist" on preparing for and placing in the National Spelling Bee.

"Instead of me asking my daughter to spell the words (many of which are unfamiliar to her), she enjoys asking *me* to spell the words. In the course of searching for a really good word to stump her mom, she visually encounters so many of the *Paideia* dictionary (the specialized dictionary of the official spelling words for the preliminary bees) words that they become more familiar to her. The *Paideia* dictionary is so handy, with the pronunciations, definitions, and language of origin right there.

"One thing that is great about this way of practicing spelling together is that it leaves me free to get household tasks done at the same time. If I were to ask her the words from the *Paideia* dictionary my hands and eyes would have to be engaged in the process of holding the dictionary and looking through it. When she asks me the words, I'm free to get other things accomplished at the same time. This way of learning spelling is really fun: I enjoy the challenge and she enjoys seeing that nobody's perfect, watching her mom make mistakes sometimes. This way of learning spelling is so much less threatening than the traditional parent-drilling-the-child approach.

"My philosophy is that it's very important for children to learn that making mistakes is part of learning, and it's good for kids to see their parents learning and that means sometimes seeing their parents make

(continues)

NATIONAL SPELLING BEE WINNER FAMILY (continued)

mistakes. Our approach is great for visual learners because they get so much visual exposure to the words, right along with their definitions. When I'm not sure about a word, I often ask her to make up a sentence for me to clarify the word. Composing that sentence is a great mental exercise for her, too. It really makes her think about what the word means and how it might be used.

"Another game my daughter enjoys playing with me while we're doing this is asking me to guess from what *Paideia* category the words come. The week before Thanksgiving, Catherine, Alison and I were back down in Washington, D.C., to visit my parents. Catherine decided to use the *Paideia* dictionary to conduct a spelling bee among the four of us (Alison, my parents, and me). She had a great time playing the "Doctor Cameron" role and choosing good words for us. In case you're wondering who won that informal family bee—well, by the time we left D.C. my parents had been eliminated, and Alison and I are still in the runoff. (Note that Alison got a handicap: Catherine only gave her words from the five new *Paideia* categories while my parents and I got words from all the categories, both old and new.) Both Alison and I have misspelled some words, but we did so in the same rounds, so the two of us are still in friendly contention!"

by your child, and can change a parent's notion of "I can't teach my child" into "I *can* facilitate my child's learning—and will!"

More Perks of Facilitating Learning

If you like what you've read so far, hang on. We're just getting warmed up.

FACILITATING USES MULTITASKING

As you've seen in the many suggested activities in this book, facilitating learning readily integrates into family life. For instance, if you're helping your child figure out multiplication by setting the table (if each of four place settings gets three utensils, how many utensils in all?), you're not only placing multiplication into a real-life context, you're multitasking! The "lesson" is brief, brilliant, and gone, to be repeated similarly tomorrow for another two minutes. It's amazing how quickly children catch on to concepts presented this way. If instead you chose to "teach" multiplication, likely you and your child would spend a larger chunk of time doing nothing *but* multiplication. In today's busy households, facilitating learning just makes sense.

FACILITATING STRENGTHENS FAMILY TIES

We've discussed the benefits to your child of forming social learning relationships with adults in general and mentors specifically. There's no reason you can't fit into this category. I'm not talking about becoming your child's best buddy but a trusted and respected guide because your experience is valuable and your attention priceless. At the same time, you are trusting and respecting your child in return. This two-way street builds strong relationships that last through the years.

FACILITATING DEVELOPS THINKING SKILLS

When we rely on our memories of school as we think about teaching, we picture a possessor of knowledge dispensing information and answering students' questions. When we think of aiding the learning process, we turn things around. Instead of giving information our child may or may not have asked for, we guide him, often by *asking* questions, to figure out the sources of information he's looking for, remove roadblocks to his obtaining them, and allow him to *discover*. It's the act of seeking and discovering, not the content of the information that is important. (This is why it doesn't matter what the topic of research is.) He will only need to experience this a few times before he can readily transfer his thinking skills to any endeavor, making him a more effective student.

FACILITATING ALLOWS ROOM FOR CUSTOMIZATION

In order to be able to dispense information, a teacher must have a prepared agenda, likely one of the more frightening aspects of picturing ourselves as teachers. Not so for a learning facilitator who, as a matter of course in her learning lifestyle, watches for those learning opportunities that life provides every day. Because you know your child and her learning style so well, you're not trying to create learning, you're helping learning to unfold. Example? Your child is having trouble remembering all the dates associated with the Civil War that he knows are going to be on the test. Is he into rap music? Help him put together a rap song that incorporates the dates. Is she a visual learner? Make a time line. Kinesthetic? Put each date on a sheet of paper and spread them across the living room floor. Then have your child literally jump on the right answer to a question.

FACILITATING LETS US PAY ATTENTION TO PERSONAL GROWTH

When we focus on simply dispensing information, we don't allow ourselves many alternatives to figuring out the child's progress except by comparison to other students or to a predetermined "norm" for a child of that age. Once again, let's flip the perspective around to *aiding* an individual learner and her intellectual growth. When you act as your child's facilitator, you learn that comparison to others no longer makes sense. Your goal is no longer to see how much dispensed information filled the container (the brain) but to keep the child moving forward on her own growth path.

Comparisons also encourage negative labels. Even the youngest children quickly get a handle on what all the educational labels and groupings really mean. In first grade a quick glance at who is in the Bluebirds reading group reveals who the "smart" kids are. As facilitator instead of teacher, you can give your child a welcome respite from these daily comparisons. Now when you say, "Always do your best," it really means something. In addition, you relieve some of the pressure that accompanies negative labels. (Positive labels can also cause problems, particularly when children begin to feel superior to others or that they are in some way entitled to special/different treatment.)

FACILITATING ENCOURAGES AUTONOMY

Aiding a child in the learning process means just that. It doesn't mean doing it for her. A true education is achieved through experience, and the sooner your student understands this, the better equipped for academic study, as well as adulthood, she will be. The hierarchical relationship of a teacher and student encourages the student to become dependent upon the teacher for the very same information and answers the exceptional student learns how to find for herself.

As a facilitator you *don't* provide answers, you *don't* dispense information. You *are* helping to create an autonomous, self-directing student who knows how to track down the information she needs instead of waiting for someone to give it to her. An autonomous student is able to answer questions because she has a facilitator asking them.

Sharpen Your Facilitator Skills

The next two chapters discuss more aspects of facilitating learning. Right now we'll take a look at just a few of the basics that experienced learning lifestyle parents say are some of the most important lessons they've learned. Let their discoveries help get your family off to a running start!

THE ANNOYING TEACHING TECHNIQUE
EVERY PARENT SHOULD AVOID

I've seen teachers lecturing to a group of children who are obviously interested and attentive, some clearly engrossed, perhaps picturing the subject being discussed, perhaps a museum exhibit. The teacher is having exactly the effect she wants. But then she suddenly feels it's time to "involve" the children. She stops the story and asks a question like, "And where did the artist live?"

You can see on the children's faces they have been suddenly interrupted from a journey of the imagination they had been on. They're silent. They're slightly stunned. They know the answer, but they just want to get back to the journey.

The teacher waits impatiently. She's not budging. Finally, someone blurts out the answer so they can get on with it. "Yes! Belgium!" the teacher says and hopefully carries on with her story without adding yet another question, such as, "And why is that important to know?"

This methodology disturbs the flow of information and literally shuts down the thinking process while it's in gear, making the student reorient his imagination to get back to where it was before the interruption. We've all been annoyed by this teaching technique, and yet it survives from generation to generation. This is the kind of thing it's best not to bring into your home.

Lillian Jones, Sebastopol, California

AWARENESS

In chapter 2 we suggested you spend as much time as possible observing your child. The need for observation is worth mentioning again in connection with your role as a learning facilitator. You have all the qualifications you need as a facilitator: love for your child and life experience to share. Your child gives all the clues you require, visible to someone who bothers to look—and listen. By looking and listening, you become increasingly aware of the many facets of your child. Your knowledge in this area is essential for becoming the most effective aide you can be.

This next example involves a three-year-old, but the idea is the same no matter the age of the child. Ever since I became an empty nester, my granddaughter has constantly asked if I am alone when I talk with her by phone, if I will be alone when she leaves after a visit, if my younger son will be moving back. I've told her I'm fine alone, but the fact that she kept asking about it told me I wasn't getting to the source of her curiosity. One day, in preparing for a trip together, her mother and I wanted to run some things out to the car, momentarily leaving my granddaughter alone in their apartment (with the door open and the car right in front of the door). She asked us not to leave her, then began to cry. I'd never known she was so afraid to be alone. Because I witnessed this incident, the next time she questioned my being alone, I knelt down, looked her in the eyes, and told her I wasn't afraid to be alone and that I don't cry or feel at all upset when I am. She hasn't asked about it since. Staying aware of my granddaughter's behavior, feelings, and words allowed me to connect seemingly disparate clues to figure out exactly what she needed to learn.

REMEMBER, ALL LEARNING IS INTERDEPENDENT

When we think in terms of school, we think about a session of math, followed by some history, followed by science. Think in terms of facilitating within the context of a learning lifestyle, and we quickly realize one can't learn about social studies without reading, one can't study science without incorporating at least some mathematics, and what would history be like without geographic awareness?

"Trying to compartmentalize subjects can make things boring and unnecessarily complex," says www.besthomeschooling.org

creator Lillian Jones. "Math is part of everything around us; reading is more rewarding and educational when it involves interesting material; science isn't some dry set of academic subjects, but rather the language for what's happening in and around us all the time. If we divide everything up into 'subjects' we can manage to make anything seem dull and uninviting, thereby dulling the mind's natural curiosity and deeper pursuit of knowledge about a subject."

Use your time with your child to introduce her to or remind her of the concept of interconnection. "Let's take math and history," Lillian continues. "We found good children's books about the history of mathematics which, of course, is tied into the history of civilization. My son and I were fascinated to see how counting developed and evolved into more sophisticated and intricate ways of dealing with computation, and how people first learned methods for calculating the size of mountains or buildings. Who invented the use of decimals? Geometry? Finding these things out with your child is lots of fun. And," Lillian adds, "you can duplicate some of the ancient techniques with simple materials. It's also helpful to realize that math is a living way of thinking, a way of figuring things out, rather than just a set of carved-in-stone methods taught by a textbook."

SHOW, DON'T TELL

Whoever first said, "Actions speak louder than words" was a very wise soul. As a learning facilitator, you'll want to be a living model of enjoying learning, not simply its loudest cheerleader. "Kids are talked to death," says Carol Narigon, a homeschooler for a decade. "They get a constant barrage of chatter from their teachers, television, radio, their friends, and us." (So *that's* why my own children could never understand why people actually pay to hear me talk.)

Instead of talking and talking about fractions, get out the measuring cups. "If you play with water or rice or sand, it only

A TEACHER–FACILITATOR COMPARISON

Teacher	Facilitator
Hierarchical leader	Partner
Dispenses information	Helps student find information
Answers questions	Asks questions
Determines the learning agenda	Customizes the learning agenda
Measures progress in relation to other students and/or "the norm"	Measures progress by personal growth
Encourages dependence	Encourages autonomy

takes a few minutes to learn ¼ times 2 = ½," Carol explains. "Worksheets take much longer and *still* don't show a kid why fractions are important. To cement the knowledge, bake some cookies and divide them equally between you."

There are other ways to show instead of tell. "Don't try to make your child learn things you wish you had learned," Carol warns. "If you want him to play a musical instrument, learn to play one yourself, or get out your old violin. Take piano lessons together. Yes, he'll probably learn it quicker than you; let him help you." Carol continues: "Don't be a stage mom. Take a theater class or audition for a play yourself. Join a softball team instead of insisting your child play T-ball. Don't live through your child, but show him a well-rounded, fulfilled life through example."

In addition, it isn't wise to tell your child to do things you don't want to do. "Instead of asking why she doesn't write a letter to grandma, write a letter to grandma yourself and ask if she'd like to include a note or a picture in the envelope," says Carol. "Do it regularly. It will pay off later if she moves away from you."

Let's Hear It for Parental Involvement

"Homeschooling's most important lesson is that parental involvement is essential to a child's academic success," former Secretary of Education William Bennett told Becky Mollenkamp for "Learning from Homeschool Families," her August 2002 *Better Homes and Gardens* article. "Homeschoolers are able to wear the education hat most of the day," Bennett continues. "But all parents can put that hat on for at least a few minutes a day."

Sure, there will be things you don't know. But as learning partners who are constantly increasing your ability to find information, you and your child can discover the answers together. Since you're reading this book, the question is not *if* you're going to don that hat Bill Bennett talks about, but which one? It may feel odd at first, but do try on the facilitator hat. Ah, yes. As a parent, it becomes you!

CHAPTER 12

For Thinking Out Loud

I F WE WANT OUR CHILDREN to learn how to make a bed, we show them how to make a bed. If our children want to learn how to throw a baseball, we show them how to throw a baseball. If we want them to learn how to think, what should we do?

Show them how it's done, of course! There aren't too many skills more important to improve a child's academic performance than learning how to think. It's another of those basic skills your child will use over and over again, transferring what he learns at home with his facilitator to every subject he touches at school.

"Without being melodramatic," says Dr. Arnold Scheibel, "I think it would be very important to tell parents they are participating with the physical development of their youngsters' brains to the degree that they interact with them, communicate with them." Dr. Scheibel is the coauthor of a preliminary study on postnatal development of the brain's motor speech area, and his work is reported in Jane Healy's *Endangered Minds*. He goes on to say, "Language interaction is actually building tissue in their brains—so it's also helping build youngsters' futures."

I think of it as "brain exercise," building the muscle needed for heavy-duty thinking, reasoning, analyzing, and, yes, even day-dreaming. There's probably no simpler, more effective, easy-to-fit-into-your-lifestyle way to encourage and guide your child toward becoming the Arnold Schwarzenegger (am I dating my-self?) of the mental playground than by "thinking out loud."

Well, Yes, This Discovery *Was* an Accident

I'm one of those people whose mind pretty much stays in over-drive, so for as long as I can remember I have talked to myself—and to the dog, the television screen, the radio, Mother Nature (I affectionately refer to her as "Mama"), tiny babies, computers, and appliances that aren't working, whether they're listening or not. It was only natural that when my three children and I began home-schooling, I talked aloud in response to books, educational videos, and the incomprehensible directions for science experiments.

Talking aloud drew responses from the children, my favorite being, "Why do you say that?" Before we knew it, an hour or two had often flown by, so engrossed in conversation had we become or so intently were we seeking answers to the questions born of our discussions.

I thought aloud throughout the day. It didn't matter to me if my thoughts were related to typical school subjects or not. "I wonder if one package of spinach that says it serves four will be enough or should I make two?" "I think it was very nice of Frances to let us get our mail even though the post office was really closed, don't you?" "Which should we do next, work on the diorama or give the dog a bath? Yes, working on the diorama would be more fun, but if we wait to bathe the dog will there be enough time for her to dry off outside before it gets too cold?"

I could almost watch the wheels spinning as such talk caused the children to think—comparing four servings to the number of family members (or determining they weren't going to eat spinach anyway so one box was quite enough, thank you), considering and appreciating the thoughtfulness of our postmaster, pondering the consequences of putting off washing the dog.

I'm so glad I talked to myself.

Aha, I Wasn't Alone!

It was with great relief that I saw a certain term in Ann Lahrson Fisher's *Fundamentals of Homeschooling: Notes on Successful Family Life* when I read it in order to write its foreword. There in black and white was a name for what I had been doing: thinking out loud—mental demonstration. I wasn't the only mom who had found this interesting way to stimulate growing minds as I lived a learning lifestyle. Of course, whereas I had stumbled upon the process, Ann probably knew exactly what she was doing. Let me share what she writes about it.

> It is one thing to give an effective demonstration to teach a physical skill. It is quite another task to demonstrate mental agility and reasoning power. How are children to know that we use step-by-step processes to figure things out if we do not tell them? "Thinking-out-loud" demonstrations help children understand the inner workings of their own minds.

Now that we know what to call it, let's put it to work.

Thinking Out Loud in Action

No matter how long your child's school day is and no matter how many hours you spend at work, what's remarkable about thinking out loud is that every parent can do it every day while going about the business of life with her child(ren). To create more time and opportunity, speak with the teacher about filling your child's home time with something like "mental demonstration," instead of so much homework. Explain to the teacher what you mean. (That will sound so much more acceptable to the teacher than calling it "talking to yourself," won't it?) This is yet another interesting, fun, non-time-consuming way to learn, no complicated educational formula necessary.

Carol Narigon, homeschooling mom in Dayton, Ohio, found that "walks during which I wondered aloud to myself work most effectively when the kids are within earshot." It's simple to get started, says this *Home Education Magazine* columnist and editor. "I wonder why this tree needs long thorns on its branches? I wonder what kind of bird is making that sound? Does it have a nest nearby? What kind of animal left this track? What might its feet look like?"

After ten years of the learning lifestyle, Carol knows this is a great way to observe and build upon children's natural curiosity. "If your kids hear you talking to yourself and examining something on the ground or in a tree," she says, "they'll come over to see what you're doing. If you share your sense of wonder with them, they'll learn how asking questions can lead to interesting knowledge."

However, Carol warns, don't do it just for the kids. "Do it because you were born wanting to find out everything about your environment," she explains, "and because a curious child lives in your adult body if you only give her a voice. Be like that child who asked so many questions in her unquenchable thirst to understand and know her world." It must work. Carol plays the piano, recorder, and drums, sings, writes, reads voraciously, co-owns a Deck the Walls store with her husband, gardens, dries herbs, sews, crochets, and knits. She has a degree in social work, is a Girl Scout leader, and knows how to make anything out of polymer clay.

With younger children, mental demonstration can get downright silly, and it may even work best that way. You simply say something so outrageous to the three-to-six-year-old crowd (or thereabouts) they can't help but stop to *think* about why things are the way they are. When the door is open to this kind of talk, you are facilitating ongoing learning in a relaxed and normal way.

My granddaughter, Emily, has twin baby sisters and, along with their mom, all were at my house one day at dinnertime. As always, Emily volunteered to set the table. When she was done, I asked her how many plates she had put out. She walked back to the table to count them. "Three."

"Three. Who are they for?" I asked.

"You and Mommy and me."

"Yes, that's three, but what about the babies? They have to have dinner, too!" Emily stopped dead in her tracks, and she wore a puzzled look that meant she wasn't quite sure what to make of what I was saying.

"They drink milk," my granddaughter told me.

"Sure, they can have a glass of milk," I assured her, "but they have to eat some spaghetti, too!"

She looked at her mom for support. "They can't have spaghetti—*can* they?"

"No," her mom answered. "You're right. They still just have milk."

"They can't have spaghetti," my granddaughter stated authoritatively.

"Oh!" I exclaimed. "Is that why you only put three plates on the table?"

She nodded.

"Well, that was really good thinking," I told her. "If you had put out two *more* plates, we would have had too few plates!" And so I created an opportunity to see if she understood the difference between too few and too many. If she didn't, I had the perfect chance to talk about it while the spaghetti boiled.

It's not a bad idea to check every once in a while if the older children are listening, and you can use silliness on them, too. If

"I'm going to put the carrots in the dishwasher" doesn't make someone at least blink, repeat it, singing, in a Shakespearean voice or, if all else fails, louder, until it does.

In Ann Lahrson Fisher's exploration of the subject, she shares the story of the power of her father's almost silent shoelace-tying demonstration. He tied slowly, waiting for Ann's small, less coordinated hands to catch up to his. Just a smidgeon of patience is helpful and rewarding, as per another example in Ann's book.

> "Do we have enough change in our pockets to buy ice cream? Let's see. Ice cream costs seventy-five cents. You have a quarter and a penny. Here is my change. How many more quarters do we need? Here is one, and we still need another. A quarter is worth twenty-five cents. Let's see if we can make that value with these dimes and pennies." You let your child know there is no big mystery to the process of counting change and making purchases. Later, when he begins to grasp these ideas, he can take them over for you when you haul out your fistful of change.

Wonder about everything aloud. Encourage your child to share her opinion. At the same time you're thinking out loud you're involving your child in the decision-making process and giving her ownership of the actual decisions. Have you ever seen a child's face light up at being included in "grown-up stuff"? (This includes big children, too.) Inclusion is quite a morale booster.

One Caution About Thinking Out Loud

Engage in this activity at your own risk. Make sure you sharpen your own thinking skills and think ahead before you speak. Many parents, having just been outwitted, out-logicked, and/or out-debated by a twelve-year-old, have been heard to say, "I know I wanted her to be an independent thinker—but so soon?"

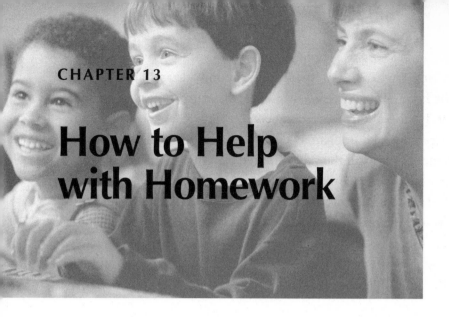

CHAPTER 13

How to Help with Homework

WHILE SOME EDUCATORS still sing the praises of homework, many parents in recent years have brought this traditional practice under intense fire. Families, already pressed for the time they need to strengthen bonds, share values, and simply enjoy each other's company, resent the intrusion into their homes of copious amounts of schoolwork. In a February 2002 special section in the *Washington Post* titled "Tonight's Assignment: Emphasize the Home in Homework," child psychologist Wendy A. Zevin points out that parents are responsible for the *whole* child, and asks, "Shouldn't we have more say about what is expected to happen in our homes? We are not usually welcome to respectfully decline or alter homework to flexibly fit circumstances."

Zevin's thinking is very much like that of a parent living a learning lifestyle: "We need a curriculum that recognizes preparing a family meal together teaches organization skills, health and nutrition, money math, recipe math (crucial fractions), cooking chemistry, reading, responsibility, teamwork and actually could be family-friendly . . . These days, the sources of stress are many and varied, carrying more combustible charges in the post-September-11 ambient anxiety. We have to remember the importance of play and the value of interest in things other than school. And that homework should not always come first."

More and more parents, convinced of the truth in Zevin's words, are talking with each other about the homework dilemma. Getting the school to change its policy across the board is likely a losing battle. However, there are incremental steps you can take. Just keep thinking outside the box—out loud, of course.

Get Your Child's Teacher on Your Team

Most human beings don't like having their "territory," or specialty, usurped. Even so, any teacher who has studied how children learn is aware that one-on-one tutoring is unquestionably the most effective way to help anybody learn anything. Make this the crux of your line of reasoning as you prepare your child's teacher to become part of your family's educational team.

Because you're aware of the teacher's learning goals for the year, you will have planned enrichment activities to go along with them. Share them! There's nothing like a well-thought-out plan to sway even the most skeptical folks that you have given deep thought to what you are proposing and that your heart is in the right place. This *is* your child we're talking about, after all.

Remember, different personalities will react to your efforts in dissimilar ways. There's no use butting your head against a wall if, after you make reasonable attempts, the teacher doesn't understand what you are trying to accomplish. You most certainly can continue your efforts without the teacher's help.

There is also safety in numbers. If you and other like-minded parents can make your case, the school will find it increasingly difficult to deny your wishes. Indeed, a second line of reasoning you and your friends might use with your child's teacher is the much-touted desire for parental involvement. One caveat: This line of reasoning can become hairy. As you might imagine, there is no greater degree of parental involvement in education than with homeschooling, yet homeschoolers face a constant barrage of criticism for their efforts. Let common sense—and your assessment of the personalities at hand—guide your decision as to how far you will press this point.

Let Your Computer Help

Even as some children are taught the basic subjects in school in much the same fashion you remember from your school days, a good number of children are learning the same skills and information via exercises and fun games on their computers. The software that accomplishes this task is called "edutainment." Not all of it is worthwhile, but the good stuff is colorful, action-packed, interactive, and plain ol' fun.

There is nothing your child needs or wants to know that can't be found with a Google search (www.google.com) of the Internet. Yes, there's a lot of junk out there in cyberspace, and I recommend filtering software whether or not your child will be surfing alone. But the Internet is also home to an amount of global information that only one decade ago was inconceivable. Let the Internet help you help your child. Your child will discover just how much there is to know about, broadening her learning horizons and empowering her to take more control of her own education.

Provide the Place

I know you've heard this piece of advice from every purveyor of "homework help," but I don't want to leave out such an obvious suggestion. Provide your child with a comfortable, well-lit, and

BE A HOMEWORK GENIE

After six to eight hours of school as usual and another two to three hours of extracurricular activities, the most important gifts you can give your children as they strive to complete daily assignments are time, space, and support.

- *Time.* Give your children time to relax so they can prioritize the next tasks after an already-busy day's schedule. Many children need "down time" before they can go forward and tackle homework assignments. It is up to you to protect this time by not overbooking their day.

- *Space.* Create a space that is comfortable and equipped with materials to stimulate creativity as well as basic reference books to assist in the completion of at-home projects (assorted paper, pencils, glue, scissors, markers, erasers, ruler, dictionary, thesaurus, grammar book, encyclopedia, atlas, etc.).

quiet (or not) place to study and tackle homework. Earlier, we discussed customizing this space, so enough said.

Help Free Your Child from Stereotypes

Believe it or not, your ability to "counter-stereotype" will help as much with homework as sitting down with math worksheets every night for three years.

- *Support.* Most important, be available! You need not be looking over their shoulder but when your children rub the lamp, you need to appear! If you can't physically be present, be sure your children know how to reach you by phone. Check in periodically. Your undivided attention is crucial! Your children must "own" their homework, but that doesn't mean they should be left alone to fend for themselves. Be on hand to help clarify teacher instructions, suggest resources, discuss concepts, and offer encouragement. You don't need to know all the answers but you should be available to say, "Let's go find out" or "Who can we ask?" A simple phone call to the teacher for clarification or visit to the library for research will help your children succeed.

Be a homework genie by anticipating your children's needs and facilitating a positive after-school environment where they can relax, feel empowered, and be supported.

All children have genius! For more information on how to discover, nurture, and protect your child's unique genius check out *Genie U: "A safe haven for your child's genius"* www.genieu.com.

Sherri Lander Smith

Freedom from school-based stereotypes is a vital contributing factor to homeschooled children's success. "This increases their ability to develop into their own person," explains Ann Lahrson Fisher, mother of two grown, homeschooled daughters, "rather than the 'type' of person they are classified to be by their schoolmates."

Homeschooled children who later attend school are often more aware of classification because they have spent some time without it. They report that they have to struggle to remain free of it. If it's this difficult for those who guard against it, it must be harder for those who aren't aware it's happening. If you don't know what other children say about your child at school, find out.

"Pretty doesn't equal stupid, for example," Ann continues. "Liking sports doesn't make you a jock. The so-called 'normal' teen peer groups that develop in school are not that normal in that they don't exist anywhere else in society, and they often result in teens with an underdeveloped sense of self." Many children who get negative labels obliviously live up to them, subconsciously sabotaging themselves at the starting gate. In some schools it's not cool to be smart, so children learn to hide intellectual gifts rather than face the ridicule of others. What you don't use, you lose.

As the parent, you are in the best position to counter any negative influences of stereotyping. You will do this by allowing your child the opportunity, space, and time to discover who she really is by surrounding her with people and an environment that are supportive. In addition, the negative effects, says Ann, "can be diminished by schooling families with family togetherness; summer family trips, social activities, independent and group travel, and much more."

The Individualized Education Plan (IEP)

We'll soon address homework help for students stumbling over a specific problem as well as those who have to struggle a bit harder in general. First, here's something that's a benefit to all children. It's an individualized education plan, known as an IEP in school talk. Because they are partners in the experience, many homeschooling parents and children formulate an IEP, which serves as a map of the learning road ahead. You and your child can create an IEP at the beginning of the school year, revisit it regularly, and tweak or entirely rewrite it as needs and opportunities change.

Federal law requires that schools prepare IEPs for special education students, and some districts also create plans for students in gifted programs. It is also common sense to prepare individualized plans for the children in the middle, and some schools in Maryland, Vermont, and Virginia, along with Washington's Twin Lakes Elementary School, have begun to do this.

In a December 10, 2002, article for the *Seattle Times,* reporter Matthew Craft explains these IEPs for regular students. He says they are not as detailed and therefore not as time consuming for teachers as are the special education plans. One teacher reported she spent only four hours writing plans for sixteen students. "The IEPs," writes Craft, "involve getting parents, teacher and student to draw up a list of goals and ways to reach them." Depending on individual children's needs, "parents might be asked to keep an eye on their child's homework, or make sure they read for thirty minutes every night."

At Seattle's Lawton Elementary School, parents may request a plan. "We know that individualized instruction is the best way to get kids to achieve," Principal Sylvia Haden says. "When you have kids at different levels, with different learning styles, you can't treat them all the same."

Reporter Craft tells of one student diagnosed with Attention Deficit Disorder whose reading scores were below grade level. Then, last year, the boy started hitting targets on the reading test. His mother credits his IEP begun in first grade. "With the learning plan, we knew what the teacher was doing and we know what we can do," she said. "As a parent, you're informed early on; you're made part of the solution."

If your child's school doesn't recognize the value of individualized education, you and your child can make an IEP yourselves.

Like the school in Craft's report, keep it simple so as not to over-whelm your child. Just one or two goals, for a single marking period or for the entire year, can make a big difference in your child's desire to succeed and ability to focus. If need be, concentrate on one goal at a time. A goal may be anything that is realistically at-tainable yet stretches your child to new heights, whether to im-prove spelling, increase his understanding of history, or figure out geometry. The goals of an IEP need to be specific: Receive a B or better on a spelling test before the first quarter is over, learn how the Civil War changed the country, be able to correctly write the proofs for four out of five geometry problems. (Remember, you'll have checked ahead of time with the teacher about the curriculum so you will be able to make the goals as specific as possible.)

If your child is already proficient or comfortable with an up-coming curriculum, crank it up a notch and create goals above and beyond the school's requirements. Either way, once your list of goals is written down, brainstorm for ways to reach them. Use your creativity, think outside the box, keep your child's learning style in mind, and encourage suggestions from your child. In this way, you'll find a road that's right for your child and your learn-ing lifestyle. If you find yourselves stumbling, pick a different road: There are limitless ones to choose from. Hang the goals on your refrigerator or anywhere you both will see them every day.

Adjust Your Attitude

Filled with their own memories, lots of parents dread homework as much as their children do. A child readily picks up on your negative demeanor, so work on adjusting your attitude before you start to help. The old theory that if you smile and think happy thoughts you'll grow happier works here. In this case, model enthusiasm and a love of learning, and eventually you *will* find yourself with a different attitude. More important, your child will follow.

Homework Nitty-Gritty

Now that your goals are staring you in the face, your team works together to reach them. Bring your new attitude and pull up a chair.

SPECIFIC CONCEPT PROBLEMS

The self-confident child whose learning style matches the school's teaching style rarely needs help with homework. When she's stuck, it's usually a single concept that's giving her trouble. Here are a few tips to get her over (or around or through) the stumbling block. These tips are also useful for the child with greater homework difficulty.

Read Ahead So You Know
Where Your Learner Needs to Go

You've heard some variation of the joke where a child asks her parent where her baby sister came from, and the parent freaks and gives a forty-five-minute biology talk. Then the child says, "Oh, Danny's new brother just came from the hospital."

We parents often resort to overkill when it's unnecessary. The parent in the joke could have saved some time if she knew where the child was going with her question. Knowing where your child has to go *after* he gets past the stumbling block can help you figure out not only how to get around it but also how important it is in the greater scheme of things. If your child is working from a textbook or other written material, you can read ahead and get a good idea of how detailed the study will become.

One common stumbling block for me in school was Roman numerals. A quick glance in the textbook would have shown me that within a week the class and I would march on to an entirely different skill, because Roman numerals covered only five pages. But look at this. The chapter on long division coming up would go on for more than thirty pages. If I had looked ahead, I would have known that in the "big picture" Roman numerals played a small part, and I could have relaxed accordingly and kept this difficulty in perspective! (*The Ultimate Book of Homeschooling Ideas* has several Roman numeral games you can play at home, in the car, or on the beach that will probably convey the basics within a week.) Judging by the amount of space given over to these numerals, I could have realized that any major test would likely only have a couple of numeral-related questions, and getting them wrong wouldn't send me to the bottom of the class.

Use some of the methods below to kick your child's stumbling block out of the way. If the block won't budge, let it go, and work on the concept for five or ten minutes each day for the next week.

But what if your child is having trouble with that more intense long division instead? You've looked ahead so you understand getting this concept is pretty important. Knowing this gives you and your child the opportunity to figure out how to devote a bit more time to it, and you can plan to adjust your schedules, if necessary. (Remember this stumbling block, too, shall pass, so any schedule change is only temporary.) You know this concept is worth getting more information about from the library or the Internet, or enlisting your math genius husband or someone else for a brief tutoring stint. Helping with homework doesn't necessarily mean you have to do it all yourself.

Watch your child try a few problems to discover where she's going wrong. Start from there. Really listen to her explanation of her difficulty so you can focus on it, instead of giving the equivalent of the joke's biology lesson when all you have to say is, "You subtract that."

Explain It Differently

If your child isn't getting a concept in school, chances are that more of the same teaching method at home isn't going to work, either. However, you can try, as your close relationship with your child does alter the approach somewhat. If you see it's still not working, don't keep banging your head against the same brick wall or driving your child to tears.

Instead, present the material in a completely different context, which is a great idea at any time, not just with a homework problem. In fact, the editors of *How People Learn: Brain, Mind, Experience, and School* found "knowledge taught in a single context is less subject to transfer than knowledge acquired through a variety of contexts." As we've seen, this means the process of learning needs to be considered along with content. Children are more likely to hang onto the relevant features of concepts when the material is presented in multiple contexts (just as it is in natural contexts). As a bonus, multiple-context presentation also increases understanding of how and when to put knowledge to use (called "conditions of applicability").

So think of some real-life examples of the concept in action and get going! Use manipulatives. Phrase questions in terms of family members, pets, or favorite toys. Give the information relevance to your child. If you give him something to "hang it on," the information will stick. Or put it in context with the next suggestion.

Don't Coerce, Divert!

Building on the "thinking-out-loud" idea in the previous chapter, author Ann Lahrson Fisher's husband coined the phrase "joyful disruptions" that nicely expands this idea into the realm of homework help (see more at www.nettlepatch.net /homeschool). Ann writes:

> Yes, you can be ridiculous while working on academics. Silliness can ease the struggle to understand tough concepts for many youngsters.
>
> Suppose your child is in the early stages of learning fractions. He comes up to you beaming with satisfaction. He has done an entire page of problems without even being told how to work them. And every single problem, you notice, is wrong. Suppose he made a common beginner's

error, adding numerators to numerators and denominators to denominators, with this result: $\frac{1}{2} + \frac{1}{2} = \frac{2}{4}$. He has given you a key piece of information about where he is in his understanding of fractions and wholes. You might simply hand the paper back and say, "Can you figure out what you did wrong?" Or you could smile absentmindedly and pretend that you didn't notice that the problems were wrong, knowing he'll catch on when you review next month. Or you may decide you have some reteaching to do.

Or you can use a joyful disruption. By doing so, you can playfully help him learn, let him down gently, and minimize frustration, feeling stupid, or being embarrassed.

Try something like this. "Very cool. You are doing Slimegonian fractions. In Slimegonia, they have a rule of adding denominators and numerators just like you did. Guess what else? Kids grow up ve-e-e-ry slowly in Slimegonia. They grow for $\frac{1}{2}$ year, and then for another $\frac{1}{2}$ year, and they are still only $\frac{1}{2}$ year older, just like in your problem!"

If he hasn't figured out what you are getting at yet, create some more nonsense with another example. "Oh, yeah, and in Slimegonia, it is impossible to double a recipe! All Slimegonian math is done in fractions, you see, so even if they needed two cups of something, it would say $8/8 + 8/8$, and guess what the answer would be?"

At whatever point you child tires of silliness or begins to see the light, move to Earth math.

HELPING THE STRUGGLER

Some children face a homework minefield instead of an occasional stumbling block. Often, this indicates the child wandered off the learning path some time ago and needs help finding his way back on. This problem runs deeper than a single challenging concept, so it requires additional attention.

Study the Big Picture

There are so many ways that a child can detour off the learning road. If this is the case, it's important to know how and where the

From One Parent to Another

Toward Joyful Reading

I knew a little about the way Waldorf reading was taught, so I did my own version of that, where I drew pretty crayoned pictures of each letter, using those beautiful beeswax crayons, making up a (in my case) silly little story that went along with the sound. The "k" turned into a king, for instance. This was simply an introduction, no drilling or writing. We messed around like that for a while, and then I took him to a tutor (a retired kindergarten teacher) who did something I could have done if I had realized it at the time. She simply went over the letters with some little games and showed him how the letters get pronounced in a pushed-together, rather than individual, way for words, which is probably the trickiest part of all.

Then the teacher introduced him to the Mac and Tab books, cute little booklets that each concentrate on a few letters. Example: Mac has a Pal. So now he could read a cute little story in each booklet. That's how we did it. But I've heard of many, many children who have picked up reading quite naturally from being read to while the parent moves a finger along under the words—or a variety of other ways.

My son happened to be the kind of learner who clicked in well with the method I assumed, for lack of knowledge of anything else, he needed. About a year later I discovered he had taught himself to read complex, multisyllable words from poring over his Nintendo strategy magazines. This is a very common story that I've heard from other moms. He had an interest that drew out a natural ability to learn that we're all born with. We don't all learn the same way, but we all have our methods of learning. Oftentimes our own methods of learning get stuffed down and muffled, because other people are so busy trying to tell us how to learn!

Lillian Jones

detour happened. The problem may have nonacademic roots. Possibilities include a bad teacher or a personality conflict with the teacher. Is it possible to speak with the teacher or change the child to a different class? It could be stress or other negative emotions in the child's personal life. You will need to find the cause and address it. Perhaps your child's learning style doesn't lend itself to comprehending a particular subject. In the home environment, try alternatives that allow him to use his intellectual strengths. She may have been made fun of for being too smart or too stupid or the teacher's pet. Spend more time helping her get out of her stereotypical role. Or the detour might be just a general decline in interest in learning as he ages. Focus on making learning fun again.

Each of these causes requires a different "fix." When time with your child is precious and limited, knowing the cause of struggle allows you to focus your time and energy where it's most needed. Notice, too, that when you look at the big picture to search for a cause, the answer isn't necessarily more homework, more worksheets, or solving fifty problems instead of twenty.

You may discover, though, the problem does have academic roots. That is, your child either failed to learn or was never taught (and if she failed to learn that really means she was never taught, doesn't it?) the skills and/or knowledge necessary to accomplish the task before her. You're going to get the same results as if you told *me* to put a new transmission in your car.

You can find where your child needs to reenter the learning road by observing the big picture. Determine the point by incrementally "backing up" through material, not by tests, but through conversation, questions, thinking out loud, and joyful disruptions, much the same way you would figure out where a coworker dropped the ball so you can provide him with the information necessary to do it right next time.

A child missing basic skills will move closer to academic success by spending time receiving these skills, not by memorizing facts or trying to cram information that, without a skills founda-

HOW TO HELP
WITH HOMEWORK

- Get your child's teacher on your team

- Let your computer help with edutainment and readily available information

- Provide a comfortable, well-lit, quiet (or not) place for study

- Help free your child from stereotypes

- Create an Individualized Education Plan (IEP) with your child and her teacher, if possible

- Adjust your own attitude about homework

- Read ahead so you know where your child is going

- Explain it differently, because if one way isn't working, it's doubtful more of the same will help

- Use "joyful disruptions" to make learning and inevitable mistakes more fun and enjoyable

- Study the big picture to determine where your child stumbled off the learning road and discover basic skills that may be missing

- Form a homework cooperative

tion, will disappear quickly. Here are just a few samples of strengthening skills while using the big picture.

- Math or reading analysis skills—Learn to play chess.

- Trouble with foreign language—In many colleges learning American Sign Language counts as study of a foreign language and it's easy to learn at home. Check with the colleges and universities your child wants to attend for details.

- Slow or uninspired reading—Use your knowledge of your child's interests to obtain material so interesting he can't resist, then just leave it around the house.

- Resistance to learning to read or reading out loud—One homeschooling mom's son gathered Beanie Babies to sit with them as they took turns reading. Her son played himself and a couple of Beanie Babies, and mom was often a Beanie Baby reader, too. Each of the Beanies had a personality and different reading skills. All of the Beanies read less well than the boy, so the pressure was off. Some of them made horrible mistakes, or threw tantrums, or obnoxiously corrected each other (all via the boy). Mom reports he now reads for enjoyment for hours each day— minus the Beanies. (Adapted from *The Ultimate Book of Homeschooling Ideas.*)

- Spelling skills—Instead of regular letters or writing, use sign language, radio code (alpha, bravo, Charlie, etc.), or dry erase markers on the window.

- Science—Practice the scientific method. One mom purchased small bags of three different types of M&M's, explained the scientific method, and conducted "an experiment." She asked her child several questions before (these were his estimates) and after (this was his research) opening the bags. Questions included: Which bag has the most M&M's? Which candies are biggest? Which are smallest? How many kinds have something besides chocolate in the middle? Which bag cost the most? How many coins make 32 cents (the cost of a small bag of M&M's)? Which bag gives you the most M&M's for your money?

When finished, eat some, save some. The level of difficulty is easily changed for different aged children. (Adapted from *The Ultimate Book of Homeschooling Ideas*.)

- History and social studies—To create connections, talk about what was going on in the larger world during the time period being studied.

- Listening skills—This takes two children or your participation. Both receive the same number and sizes of pieces of Legos or other building set with duplicate pieces. Sit in such a way the two can hear, but not see, each other. One builds something from pieces, then gives verbal directions to the other so s/he can build the same thing. Take turns. Between turns, figure out what went wrong and how to communicate and listen better the next time. (Adapted from *The Ultimate Book of Homeschooling Ideas*.)

- Attention span and thinking skills—Guided by interests, use all manner of puzzles, mysteries, secret codes, treasure hunts—indoors and out, for things or information—brain teasers, riddles, magic tricks, model cars, planes, dinosaurs, and dioramas.

Because of our school experience, we're used to separating learning into numerous different compartments and hiding the interconnectedness of it all. Parents who make education a top priority have found that keeping the big picture in view at all times helps them and their children see—and benefit from—the connections. They can make corrections rapidly because problems are apparent instead of hidden.

Form a Homework Cooperative

Think your child is the only one unable to decipher algebra or spell "ostentatious?" Think again! I guarantee there are other children around with the same or similar problems who might think it's a good idea to get together and share learning strategies or activities that help build the basic skills they're missing.

You can form a "homework help" cooperative in the same way you build one of the broader learning cooperatives. In fact, you could call this a "niche" cooperative. The group can take turns meeting at different members' homes with the homeowner in charge of that meeting's activities. If your group has six members and meets twice a week, each family hosts just one meeting every three weeks. This approach is particularly effective for children with intrapersonal intelligence, but most children should find this more fun than slaving over a textbook alone.

A few more basics will help any child, especially as she gets older and the information really starts to fly. We'll visit them in the next chapter.

CHAPTER 14

A Survival Guide to Notes, Study Habits, and Test Prep

RUMOR HAD IT the class was an easy A, so of course I added it to my freshman high school year schedule. In retrospect, it was the most valuable class I ever took. It's the only class where I used what I learned through the entirety of high school and still employ the skills today.

The class was called "Personal Typing and Shorthand." Created with college preparatory students in mind, its purpose was to help us become more successful students (read: get better grades) by getting the necessary information efficiently, correctly, and in an organized manner right at the beginning of the process. The process was at that time, as it basically remains, to receive information, study it, and provide proof that you "got" it via pop quizzes, tests, essays, research papers, and projects. Even back then I didn't understand why *every* student wasn't shown these skills—even earlier in her school career. Given the nature of the school setup, these are the very tools a child needs to get the job done and to do it well.

In my consulting and tutoring work over the last twenty years, I've asked every student if anyone ever explained these skills to her. Not one has said yes. No matter the subject for which children seek my consulting help, I concentrate on them learning these skills first.

Taking and Organizing Notes

This is where the process begins. You can't give back information, whether on a test or in another form, unless you get that information in the first place. Not only do you have to get the information, you have to get it in a way it still makes sense three days, three weeks, or three months from now. The key is notes that are as complete, concise, and organized as possible. Let's explore some methods so you can help your child learn these skills at home.

SHORTHAND

This system of getting words onto paper includes simple strokes of a pen or pencil (I recommend pencil) that stand for letters, sounds, and, in some cases, entire words. I haven't heard much about Gregg or any other shorthand since dictation machines and computers came on the market, so I'm not recommending an in-depth study. However, an overview to learn just some of the strokes will help your child take notes more quickly, freeing up the time necessary to take more detailed notes or get back to listening to the teacher.

Laura Tichenor's sixteen-year-old twins are dabbling with community college, each taking two courses. "I originally dismissed the idea when Linda suggested the girls learn what I thought of as 'primitive' shorthand. I mean, it's the twenty-first century!" Laura says. "Shortly after that I went to a library book sale and there on the table was a Gregg shorthand practice book, so I spent a whole quarter on it. We 'played' with the strokes for a few days, then I shared what Linda had told me about using it for note taking."

Gregg Shorthand for Commonly Used Words

Word	Shorthand Stroke
a	•
the	(
and	)
for	)
under	⌒
over	⌣
but, be, by	(
with	ƍ
about	ℓ
were	ℓ
where	ℓ
are	⌣
they	ℓ
to	⌒
would	/
could	⌢
should	✓

The girls began experimenting and soon started looking up and learning frequently used words. "My daughter told me it was the best quarter I'd ever spent," says Laura.

Just a few useful strokes for commonly used words appear in the sidebar. More information is free for the taking on the Internet (http://www.notetaking.com has a lot of interesting links) or in books at your library. If you catch younger children while they think "secret code" is really cool, they'll find this fun and get a head start on quicker note taking. If you also learn the marks at the same time, you and your child can practice reading and writing by using shorthand in useful or funny notes to each other. Your child can make up his own shorthand system, too, if so inclined.

ABBREVIATIONS

Abbreviations save additional time. Common ones include @ for "at," w/ for "with," w/o for "without," and + for "and." Don't let your child stop there. When studying a topic, key words, terms, and phrases get repeated often. Have your child leave the first page of a notebook blank (more on notebooks coming up). This will become the page of abbreviations for the notebook. When in a hurry, she can just jot down a new abbreviation and what it stands for in the margin of the page she's working on and add it to the first page later.

Abbreviations can take whatever form makes sense to her. It's quicker to write "RW" than Revolutionary War, "I" than India, and "h" than hypotenuse. Many people worry about spelling a word right as they take notes, and this kind of fussing wastes time and diverts attention. Your child can write a word with tricky spelling just once in the margin, quickly make up an abbreviation for it, then forget it, at least until it appears on a spelling word list, that is.

NOTEBOOKS, PAPER AND OTHERWISE

If your child isn't using a computer, single-subject notebooks are a great aid to organization. Notes scribbled on three-ring-binder paper that falls out, or paper scraps tossed into a notebook for

TIPS FOR TAKING AND ORGANIZING NOTES

- Learn some basic shorthand strokes

- Abbreviate and note what the abbreviation stands for

- Use single-subject notebooks for recording

- Practice picking out the important points of a talk or lecture

- Put notes in outline form

- Clean up, fill in, and organize notes while the information is still fresh in your mind

- Type notes for neatness and additional review

- Organize your time using an assignment book

later often get lost. Single-subject notebooks also help avoid some of that back strain from heavy backpacks because notebooks can stay in the locker until needed.

Notebook computers may serve the same purpose but are only useful if your child knows how to sort and file the typed notes. Find out if she knows how to do this. If not, help her learn either with your assistance or someone else's.

What's Important to Write Down?

No one can write down *everything* the teacher says no matter how much shorthand or how many abbreviations the person uses. Successful students separate the wheat from the chaff and don't waste time writing down insignificant material.

If the class uses a textbook, reviewing the upcoming material for just a few minutes the evening before provides an important head start. Your child can get in the habit of reviewing subject headings and reading photo, chart, or map captions. She can look at the questions included in chapter reviews and figure out what the textbook writers deem important.

Interestingly, some of the best clues about what to write down come from knowing a teacher's mannerisms. Help your child learn how to "read" the teacher. In an Illinois university, Samantha Bouyea's older son Steven recognized, "While talking to a class, teachers often say what they have to say on a given point, then glance at the book or notes to check what the next point is they want to make. Typically, they make the point, then elaborate." The "point" may become an outline heading (more on outlines soon), with supporting information beneath it.

Teachers have their own individual quirks, too. "I have one teacher, for example, who always scratches his head while pondering what to bring up next," Samantha's son explains. "Another takes a deep breath as if to recharge before changing gears." If your child finds it hard to practice this "teacher-reading" skill, attend a lecture together or find one on television and observe the speaker together. Then think out loud.

OUTLINES

Ah, outlines. Boring, yes, but one of life's valuable information organizers. One Web site calls them "the shelves on which you organize your ideas and sentences." Better?

Notice the common outline format in the sidebar.

Organizing information immediately upon receipt saves a lot of time in the long run. Many children with unorganized notes spend hours cramming for a test and trying to remember it all because they can't ascertain the difference between important and less important material. In outline form, primary and secondary information is apparent, and the child has a better idea where to focus

OUTLINE FORMAT

I. Use Roman numerals (see why I had to learn them?) for main ideas

    A. Subordinate categories go here

    B. Outlines should generally have at least two entries in each of the letter/number categories. Common wisdom says if you don't have at least two, you don't need the first one.

        1. More details about "B" go here...

        2. ...and here

            a. More details about "2" go here...

            b. ...and this is the typical "depth" of information outlines reach. To go further, use

                i. Lowercase Roman numerals

                ii. And so on

attention. A misplaced piece of information, such as a teacher might give out of context, may be written in the page's margin and put in proper place when the child cleans up the notes later.

An outline can take many forms, depending on what best serves your child's needs. Sometimes a single word on a line is enough; sometimes a single word accompanied by a note that says, "see page 234" may be used for an idea too complicated to get down on paper while the lecture continues. Some children like to write in complete sentences while for others phrases suffice.

If you've discovered you've got a very visual learner, she may get better results by drawing maps or using something called "clustering." I found the clustering idea in a book called *Writing*

Cluster Notes

Students who learn better by seeing connections may benefit from a more free-flowing, visual method known as clustering.

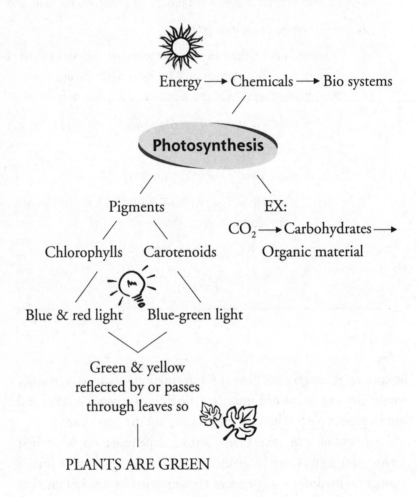

Down the Bones: Freeing the Writer Within (Shambhala Publications, 1986) by Natalie Goldberg. Intended to stimulate related thoughts for writing projects, the product, as you see above, can help a visual learner gather related ideas. It's a more freestyle method of getting the important information on paper but it, too, allows your child to see the connections and relative importance of each notation.

CLEANING UP NOTES

The child will do well who gets in the habit of typing up the day's notes, in study hall if he carries a computer, or when he returns home. Microsoft Word and other word-processing programs even recognize the formation of an outline and do half the work for him!

Because the lecture or instruction is still fresh in his mind, your child can review the notes and make any necessary changes. Perhaps an idea needs a little more fleshing out, or what he originally put down is confusing and should be written a different way. This is when your child can go back to those misplaced notes in the margin and place them where they belong.

Equally important, cleaning up the notes is an opportunity to review—quickly—the day's lessons. By doing this a few minutes each day, he'll remember the material better and have an easier time studying when the "big test" looms.

TYPING

The typing skills I picked up in high school made preparing reports and term papers that much easier, but they also helped when it came to notes. Today your child can learn the fundamentals with inexpensive software and your home computer.

"When I was younger, I couldn't understand why Mom was always guiding me to play 'Mavis Beacon Teaches Typing,'" admits Connor Johnson, a college freshman in Pennsylvania, "but once I hit the college doors I understood perfectly. When my roommate swore that his hunting-and-pecking was just as quick, we chose two paragraphs out of one of our textbooks and tested his theory," Connor recalls. "Not only did I get done faster, I had fewer mistakes . . . thanks, Mom!"

Once a child can type, she'll see that it's relatively quick and painless to type out a few pages of notes each day. She'll practice her typing skills, very valuable in the age of computers, wind up with easy-to-read notes, and will review the material *yet again* in the process of typing. How's that for multitasking?

ORGANIZING TIME
WITH AN ASSIGNMENT BOOK

Here's one notebook that should accompany your child everywhere throughout her day. A small spiral-bound (4″ × 6″ or so) notebook or day planner usually fills the bill.

This is where the successful student keeps track of everything she needs to do during the course of a day. In the old days we only wrote down school assignments, but today's children have so many extracurricular activities to attend it's a good idea to keep a running calendar of things like basketball practice, music lessons, or baby-sitting on the same page. Keeping all this information in one place helps your student organize her time.

If she sees she has a full afternoon and evening of activities on a given day, she knows this isn't the best day to talk her way through study hall period or make plans to hit the mall right after school. Better to get that big science assignment out of the way while she can. Conversely, if there's a big history test tomorrow and her evening is clear, it might be better to study for that at home and complete the twenty math problems while in study hall. Since many schools don't address time management with children, you may have to show your student how to get started and explain the rewards of the practice.

Study Habits and Test Prep

I've combined study habits and test prep in the same section because I believe effective study, as opposed to just getting homework done as quickly as possible, is valuable test preparation that lessens the need for cramming, which is really short-term memorizing rather than study. A child who actually studies will finish up knowing something, whereas the child who crams retains very little.

Many children consider homework and studying for tests a necessary evil to get over with as quickly and painlessly as possible so they don't interfere with *really* important things to do after school. I empathize and know a child who has really figured out the system can pull it off, but in most circumstances this isn't an attitude conducive to academic success.

Ask your child to think about his favorite sports team. Ask if they begin practice at eleven P.M. or only practice when they've got nothing better to do. What happens when the players don't bother preparing because they know the other team is "easy to beat"? Children of almost any age know this approach doesn't result in success. They understand the winning team practices on a schedule, doesn't procrastinate, takes a challenge seriously, and approaches a game *prepared*. Explain that the same wisdom applies to learning and your child's academic career.

Because they've already taken on as much responsibility as possible for their own education, homeschooled children who go on to traditional school and college know almost intuitively that preparation is key to success. Often, their parents have modeled or otherwise facilitated the habits that get the job done well, and you can, too.

What You Can Do to Help Your Child Get Off to the Right Start

Relax. When it comes to study and test prep, the onus is on your child, but you can see to it that she starts in the right direction.

PROVISIONS

Now that your child has the perfect place to study, there are a few provisions a serious student should always have within arm's reach. Since study, especially for older children, involves a lot of reading, a good dictionary is a must. Even though dictionaries are revised to include contemporary words, one purchased today should serve your child well for at least a decade, so don't settle for a $2.99 special. While shopping, don't forget to check out subject dictionaries, especially ones that apply to your child's interests. When my son got into song writing, our rhyming dictionary was never on the shelf!

A thesaurus is invaluable when writing papers. Has your child used the adverb "best" ten times, making his paper sound repetitive? He can try finest, utmost, topflight, top drawer, unsurpassed, superior, first-rate, choice, preeminent, peerless, unequaled, nonpareil, supreme, or tops, instead. A thesaurus also includes antonyms for many entries, and using, utilizing, applying, employing, operating, and manipulating one can't help but improve the user's vocabulary. You get the idea!

Encyclopedias, while nice to have, can get expensive and go out of date. If you have a computer, check out the many Internet offerings, some for free and some for a subscription price.

A calculator is also handy, as are a ruler, stapler, paper clips, extra pens and pencils, and protractor and compass, if appropriate.

ROUTINE

Today's hectic lifestyles make establishing a study routine challenging but not impossible. A routine doesn't have to mean the same exact time every day, especially when your child has to work around sports practice, music lessons, and scout meetings. In our case, a routine means preplanning just to make sure study happens at some point.

"I didn't think seriously about a schoolwork routine until one of my daughters woke me up at two o'clock in the morning because she'd forgotten to study for a science test," remembers Cynthia Reynolds, "and there was no getting her back to bed until I asked her the review questions. I appreciate my sleep too much to go through that again."

Each member of Cynthia's family has a different schedule every day. "I instituted 'routine' by having each of the kids call me at work as soon as they get home," Cynthia says. "They tell me what they have to do and we figure out the best way to get it all done. I haven't had to look at a science book at two in the morning since."

When thinking about a routine, take your child's predisposition into account. For some, homework and study go smoothest when tackled immediately upon returning home. Other children may find they focus better when they take a break first to wind down, grab a snack, or perform some physical activity. Some want the daylight hours for play and socializing, so save homework for after dinner, and the night owls among us do their best work after the moon comes up. If you and your child aren't sure what works best, experiment to find out.

STANDING OFFER OF HELP

We humans do *everything* better when we know our loved ones support us. Offer help to your child frequently, without becoming a nag, of course. Help doesn't mean literally doing the homework. It does mean being there if she wants to practice spelling words, learn the multiplication tables, discuss a novel, or find an idea for a paper or project.

Judging by the frequency of the question asked of homeschooling parents, there's a standing misconception that in order to help a child learn you must know it yourself first. There may be particulars at times that stump both of you, but you now know there are many ways to find answers you don't already have. The majority of the time, the help that counts the most is the kind offered in the form of support and understanding.

CONTINUE READING TO YOUR CHILD

Developing solid reading skills is essential for any child's academic success. Despite a national requirement that all children, ready or not, learn it at the same age, we forget there is still a lot of enjoyable literature that even the best younger readers can't handle themselves. Once they become competent enough to tackle it alone, often the subject matter has grown too juvenile to interest them anymore.

"What really important literature can a child under twelve read?" asks Lillian Jones. "Why not let her read whatever appeals to her on her own, but read *to* her more meaty things you both love? I read wonderful children's classics to my son until he was twelve, when the books he was interested in were suddenly becoming larger and larger and more time-consuming for me to read aloud, but easy and fast for him to digest on his own. Up until then, he had just read nonfiction books about subjects that interested him. By the time he was doing all his reading on his own, he was old enough to devour complex and meaningful material. Reading remains a favorite pastime of his, and his most important source for learning."

STUDY STUDYING

This book isn't meant to be the last word on studying, so go to your library or favorite bookstore and find one of the dozens of books about improving study. As with everything else, there's a plethora of information on the Internet just waiting for you. If studying "studying" results in just one idea that resonates with your child, your time is well spent.

What Your Child Can Do

It's her time, it's her education, it's her responsibility. Share the following ideas with your child, and *she'll* start calling you an A+ parent.

TEST HER OWN ATTENTION SPAN

This test has been an eye-opener for everyone I know who tries it. With typical reading material in front of her, have your student write down the current time, then begin to read. The first time she notices her thoughts drifting, she stops and records the time, subtracts second time from first, and sees how long she concentrated. Most people find their attention span is a lot shorter than they thought. Repeat the test occasionally as she develops the habits that improve concentration.

IMPROVE CONCENTRATION

When your child sits down to homework, what subject should he begin with? Just like adults, children concentrate better on topics of interest, so for many if not most students, the answer is to start with the topic he finds most difficult. His mind is least "tired" at the start, so he has maximum energy to concentrate when he needs it most. It's also easier to anticipate more pleasant study ahead than vice versa.

An aggressive posture also improves concentration. Some children study and do homework while lying on a bed or couch or relaxing in some other manner, and it works for them. Especially while working on topics she finds least appealing, your child can try sitting up attentively, as if she were listening to an interesting story.

If hunger pangs strike frequently, your child may want to get any necessary food and drink *first* so he's not jumping up and down for trips to the refrigerator once he begins studying. Once a snack break interrupts, it takes additional time to get back to where he left off, so accomplishing the task at hand will take longer and longer with each successive break.

If at all possible, your child should actually avoid snacking during this time. Blood normally heading for the brain gets diverted during eating to help digestion. The result is the same thing that happens to everyone after Thanksgiving dinner, just on a smaller scale. For optimum concentration, feast after, not during, study time. Taking phone calls, instant messaging, and sending and receiving e-mail are just as distracting, if not more so, as refrigerator treks.

TAKE MORE NOTES

Particularly as children grow older, their study and homework involve lots of reading. It's time to take more notes. College students who purchase their own textbooks constantly highlight vital information and put notes in the margins. To reap the same benefit, a child with a school-owned textbook has to put the information on a different piece of paper. However, once a child learns how to extract the important ideas from reading material and put it into note form, she'll save time by not having to reread the entire chapter or section looking for answers or studying for a test. Time spent now will save time down the road.

STUDY DAILY

Here's a suggestion your child will love. Study even when there's no homework assignment. It's a great time to catch up or read ahead a bit. "I found daily study particularly helpful with math, when just a one-day lull caused me to forget key information about the concept," says Connor Johnson, "and going back to it the following day felt like starting from scratch."

Your student may even find the topic isn't all that bad when the usual pressure to perform is off.

USE ACRONYMS

Our world is full of acronyms, those funny words formed from the first letters of all the words in a title, such as NASA and AARP. They make a great study tool when your child needs to remember series of information. For example, she may need to remember the last six presidents (including the current one)—Ford, Carter, Reagan, Bush, Clinton, Bush. It would be nice if the first letters of each name actually spelled something but, more often than not,

HELP FOR STUDY AND TEST PREP

You as a parent can

- Provide the tools that help your child get the job done
- Establish a routine based on a time that works best for your child
- Provide a standing offer of assistance
- Read up on study tips to share with your child

Your child can

- Test her own attention span
- Improve her concentration
- Take more notes
- Study daily, even when there is no homework
- Use acronyms as memory aids
- Edit papers out loud
- Engage in "head talk"
- Use the Four R's for tough questions
- Join or create a study group

they don't. So a little nonsense sentence is in order—"For compulsive readers, buy custom books."

EDIT PAPERS OUT LOUD

No term or research paper, book report, or essay has ever been written that couldn't be improved by editing it out loud. Your child may at first balk at the idea of sitting alone and reading out loud, or even reading a paper out loud to you, but his grade might just improve when he does. Sentences and even paragraphs may *look* perfectly fine on paper, but clumsy phrases and faulty word usage come to light when the sentences and paragraphs are *heard*.

USE "HEAD TALK"

As your child assimilates new information, encourage her to "talk in her head." It won't be new to her; you'll suggest she use what she already does in a different manner.

Remind her that when she thinks about what she should have said to the teacher, or determines how she's going to get permission to go to the party, or tries to figure out what to say to that cute boy, she talks it over in her head first. By using this same "head talk," she can discover different angles of the information she is studying, come up with questions that get her thinking more deeply about the topic, connect the information to existing knowledge, and remember it better. "Head talk" engages the brain on a different level than does reading, providing at least some of that all-important, additional context to the information.

THE FOUR R's FOR TOUGH QUESTIONS

Were the questions at the end of a section or chapter of a textbook the easiest part of your homework? They weren't of mine, and chances are they aren't the easiest part of your child's homework, either. To help him find and remember the answers, tell your child about the Four R's for tough questions.

- Rephrase—Sometimes it's just a matter of not understanding the question. Rephrase it, and the answer may become clear.

- Remember what you already know—The ability to answer this question may depend on recalling information previously given.

- Review material—If the book is asking the question, the answer is buried in there somewhere.

- Reason—What is the most logical answer?

WOULD A STUDY GROUP HELP?

While some of us need peace and quiet to think and study, others find the give and take of a group more effective. This is yet another good purpose for gathering together a cooperative of families whose children have the same need, so don't be shy. Gather them together for the benefit of all.

CHAPTER 15

When You Become the Student

YOU STAND AT A remarkable gateway. The price of entry? Love, trust, and acceptance that you have as much to learn, if not more than, your child does. When you muster up the entry fee and leap into the unknown, you receive the privilege and the honor of becoming the student. Yes, the "teacher" becomes the student! This, dear reader, just may be the most important lesson any of us will ever learn from homeschooling: It's a faith-filled leap that leads so many families toward success in academics and real life.

On Becoming the Student

Baby birds learn to fly when mama shows them how. Lion cubs learn to hunt when mama shows them how. Is it so far-fetched to think that children learn when mama (or dad) shows them how? Doesn't it make sense that becoming a motivated, inquisitive, and eager student ourselves provides our children with a daily, enthusiastic model to help them become a motivated, inquisitive, and eager student?

Being the student, as being young, is a state of mind that, once cultivated, will make your learning lifestyle as rewarding for you as it is for your child, and possibly leave you wondering how and why you waited so long.

LEARN TO SAY, "I DON'T KNOW"

My oldest child attended kindergarten before we started home-schooling. I vividly remember an early day in our learning life-style when he asked me something, and I said, "I don't know. We'll have to look it up." My answer rendered him speechless.

"What's the matter?" I asked.

"You're the teacher," he answered. "You're supposed to know everything!"

One year of half-day school attendance and my son was already possessed of conventional wisdom: The teacher has all the answers.

While many parents begin the process thinking they, too, have to know everything about everything, it usually doesn't take long before they're ready to say, "I don't know" to their naturally curious child's umpteen questions.

Not only have we been conditioned like my son to think the person in charge of our education knows all, we also learn to think somehow we are lesser human beings when we don't know it all. Then, we're embarrassed to admit it.

Admitting lack of knowledge, though, followed by an enthu-siastic, "so let's find out," is liberating. Admission frees us from the constraints of impossible perfection. Even young children, once over their shock, appreciate and embrace this honesty.

You, the student, learn that being human is more valuable to your relationship with your children than being "smarter than."

ASK QUESTIONS

When you admit you don't know everything, you open wide the door to satisfying your own growing curiosity. You're free to ask questions now! Let loose and show your child how to remain hungry for knowledge, unsatisfied with a mere taste of the story when just a little bit of digging uncovers so much more. Oh, the repercussions!

"When your children see you asking questions, they learn to dig deeper, too," says Carol Narigon. "When they dig deeper they discover many more passions in themselves than if they only skim the surface of what life has to offer. They may also build relationships with people willing to mentor them."

Do you think asking questions is making a pest out of yourself? That's what I used to think until people began telling me how much they enjoyed sharing what they know with my children and me, and how refreshing such curiosity and enthusiasm for learning was. Their response was exactly opposite what I expected.

Carol Narigon and family have also found most people love to answer questions about themselves and their work and hobbies. "One day, one of the dads in our homeschool group led a tour of the children's anesthesiology department at the Wright Patterson Air Force Base Medical Center," she remembers. "After the tour, my daughter and I were walking out with the family we'd ferried on base—another dad and two of his children—when we happened to pass the hyperbaric chamber clinic. The dad we were with is an emergency medical technician with an interest in all things medical, and he wondered, as I had before, what that chamber looked like and what they did in it."

Used to seeking ways to satisfy their curiosity, Carol and her friend entered the clinic and asked the technicians on duty if someone would show the pressure chamber to their families and explain how it works. "We ended up taking a half-hour tour of the chamber. Since no one was in it at the time, we even went inside," Carol says. "We learned as much as we wanted about wounds that won't heal, radiation exposure treatment, why deep sea divers get the bends, and how changing the atmospheric pressure around a person can help these conditions and others."

Sometimes you have to dig for the right person before you can excavate the knowledge you're after. "When you go to a zoo or museum, look for the people in the white coats or ask if a curator is available," advises Carol. "The scientists who work 'in the back' not only know about the museum's collections, they can answer specific questions in their fields as well. For example, the geologist can tell a small group about local geology and might be willing to identify some rocks from your backyard. It's much more interesting than a canned tour, but it only works if you're willing to ask questions and dig deeper."

You, the student, learn how interesting the world around you is.

LET YOUR CHILD BE THE EXPERT

Once you learn to admit to your child you don't know something, letting her take on the role of expert is easy, even fun. "Watch for signs of what lights up your child's mind," affirms Lillian Jones. "He might not be interested in standard academic subjects, but he may possess a great ability at some very specialized subject that could lead to useful fascination or toward a successful career choice. When you hear the life stories of great geniuses or simply successful people in various fields, you often find they did poorly in school but were always fascinated by what seemed obscure and useless subjects at the time. Fortunately, their parents supported them in those interests." (I never verified the story, but I remember hearing that Jim Carey, not surprisingly the class cutup, spent hours making faces in front of the mirror. Could anyone have foreseen what lay ahead for that boy?)

"This is *not* to say you should jump in on the subject and start orchestrating more study of it," Lillian explains. "To the contrary: Just be unobtrusively supportive, and let it remain the child's very own specialty rather than something he needs to perform in. Otherwise. there's a real and common danger that the parent will kill the child's interest in what might have been his passion. Rather, let him be the expert, and you be the respectful, but not overly concerned, observer."

You, the student, learn to support.

GIVE YOUR HEART TO MOTHER NATURE

Rare is the mother whose heart isn't affected as she sends her child off on his first school bus ride, or hugs him goodbye before watching his little legs climb the steps and disappear in a throng of children before the large doors slam shut.

The pervasive societal message exhorts us, "Chin up, old girl. This is the way it's supposed to be. Everybody's doing it. The kid's gotta grow up. You knew this day was coming. Push through that pain and get on the other side of it, already."

And we do keep up our chins and push through the pain, day after day, until it really does feel like this is the way it's supposed to be. At last, we've finally learned to ignore our gut, instinct, intuition, Mother Nature, whatever you want to call it, when we get certain feelings.

Living the learning lifestyle is going to help you feel again. This is how living the learning lifestyle reveals your child to you in a way other lifestyles can't. Turn over your heart to Mother Nature and allow yourself to feel those feelings. At the same time, be forewarned that allowing yourself to feel may reopen your heart to the pain you so bravely pushed away before. Pleasurable or painful, these feelings are given to you for a reason. They can intelligently guide your thoughts and actions, and they will never lead you astray.

You, the student, learn to use your valuable, innate gifts.

Enjoy Your New Life with Your Successful Child

Like many before you, right about now you may be thinking, "If helping my child achieve academic success is as easy as this sounds, a) why didn't I do this before, and b) why doesn't everybody do it?

The answer to both questions is the same. Oddly, one has to consciously seek answers to some pretty heavy-duty questions to discover that education is a relatively simple, inexpensive, family-centered, fun process. Having read this book, you are now able to uncover this information, not because of heavy-duty questions, but because of loving concern about your child's education.

Keep in mind this book would not have been published without homeschooling's continued societal acceptance, astonishing growth, and mainstream America's increasing awareness of its lengthening track record. Before that could transpire, though, a "critical mass" of parents had to discover the truths about education that I've presented in this book. While no one is certain how many families are homeschooling in America on any given day, the numbers have grown to where just about everyone knows of a homeschooling family. This removes much of the "strangeness" originally associated with the idea. People have come to realize that the homeschooling folks down the street or at church or even within their own family tree are pretty normal.

Next, the media had to pay enough attention to homeschooling success to move it from "fluke" to honest-to-goodness news. If your neighbor's doing it *and* Brian Williams is talking about it on MSNBC, and *Time* and *Newsweek* are running cover stories on it, there must be something to it.

Finally, I think America had to witness a sizeable number of homeschooled "graduates." The children had to grow up and "prove" themselves (I think this is unfortunate) by conventional means. They had to win high-profile academic contests like the National Spelling Bee and National Geography Bee. Americans had to watch them head off to college at approximately the same ratio as traditionally schooled children, then assimilate into the community. The now young adults had to get jobs, start their own businesses, and become parents, tennis and football stars, police officers and firefighters. In short, home educators had to prove the critics wrong so that others might open their minds and hearts to what homeschooling families have to say.

I sincerely thank you, for you have opened your mind and heart to read this book, and your child's life will be the richer for your having done so. Through that richer life, she steps closer to academic success. More important, through that richer life she steps closer to success measured on her terms supported by your family's values, the surest route to future happiness and security and, someday, to those of her own children.

I wish you and yours all the awakened curiosity, thrill of discovery, success, warmth, togetherness, joy, and love this beautiful lifestyle bestows upon all students, young and old.

Appendix A
Activities to Jumpstart
Critical Thinking

10 LEARNING CONVERSATION STARTERS

- What are the important things in life?

- How has using your imagination helped you solve a problem?

- What are you good at doing? What occupations would allow you to best use your skills?

- If you could have dinner with a famous artist, past or present, who would you choose? What would you discuss?

- Find an interesting court case in the newspaper and pretend you're all on the jury. Which way would you vote?

- Is it important to keep the space program going?

- Who is your favorite author? Why?

- Has the computer—and all the communication methods associated with it—helped or hindered the proper use of the English language?

- Machines are performing many calculations for us today. What are the benefits and drawbacks?

- What do you suppose is the (longest, shortest, heaviest, lightest) (animal, plant, planet, fish, person) in the world? How will we find out?

GROCERY STORE MATH

- Have your child guess what a bag of fruit weighs; weigh it to see how close she came to guessing correctly.

- If two cans cost ninety-nine cents, how much are four cans? Three?

- Guess what the total bill will be by estimating prices of items in cart while standing in check-out line.

- Estimate how many bags your groceries will fill.

- What is twenty percent of the cost of this box of cereal? How much would it be if it were twenty percent off?

- If I buy the big package of sausage links and each family member eats two per meal, how many meals will we get out of this package?

- Which is a better buy, the name brand using this coupon or the store brand without a coupon?

- How many boxes of pasta at fifty-nine cents each could you buy with $5? $10? How much change would you get each time?

- How many different deli meats would we have to buy to have three pounds if we buy one-quarter pound of each?

- Check out unit prices. Is your favorite peanut butter *really* worth that much more than the others?

- If one package contains three servings, how many packages do we need for Sunday dinner?

- How much more per pound are the red potatoes than the white?

5 FIVE MINUTE GAMES TO IMPROVE SPELLING

- What's the Word? *Have your child pick a word from the dictionary, the bigger the better. You might as well talk about the word's definition and part of speech while you're at it. Each person gets a piece of paper and writes the word at the top. Set a time limit (three to five minutes works well) for writing as many words as possible using only the letters in the big word. Use a point system depending on how many letters are in the created words (three letters = one point, four letters = two points, and so on). This can be a competition, or your child can enjoy beating his previous best score.*

- Hangman

- Edit This! *Type a paragraph or two from a newspaper, magazine, or your child's school book and make spelling mistakes. How many can she find? (Use interesting material from something she's studying for greater educational impact.)*

- One round of Boggle

- Write-A-Round. *All family members use one sheet of paper and take a turn adding a sentence to a short story that concludes with the last contributor's sentence. Have your child read story aloud when completed.*

INFORMATION YOUR LEARNER CAN USE

- Visual learner. *Put pertinent facts on poster board and hang around the house.*

- Artistic learner. *Let the artist decorate the information before hanging around the house.*

- Auditory learner. *Put information on audio tape and listen at bedtime.*

- Kinesthetic learner. *Put small amount of information next to each step so he has to hop to see next one.*

MATH GAMES

- Geoboards. *These are typically a wooden board with equally spaced nails in rows, 6 by 6, 7 by 7, and so on. The child can use rubber bands around the nails to create geometric shapes and learn about area.*

- Tangrams. *A square of material cut into seven pieces—five triangles, one rhomboid, and one square—tanagrams are used as a puzzle to recreate predetermined pictures, always using all seven pieces, or for exploring shapes.*

- Pattern blocks. *Blocks, wooden or plastic, in different colors and shapes, used for exploring patterns and shapes.*

- Monopoly

- Deck of playing cards

- Yahtzee

- Life
- Pretend store
- Add a couple of extra dice to games that require them for extra addition practice

KID-FRIENDLY ARITHMETIC EXPLORATION TURN-ONS

- Graphs. *Graphs come in all shapes and sizes and can be as colorful and complex as the creator wants. In addition, any collection of information can be graphed. Graphs open opportunities to discuss fractions (pie graphs are especially useful for this), percentages, greater than and less than, comparing, sorting, statistics, and so forth. Many computer programs create graphs, and this can lead into spreadsheets for older children.*

- Extreme Numbers. *Although lots of kids get a kick out of wildly large numbers (what's a googol?), introducing them to the other end of the scale can be equally interesting. Extreme numbers abound—plain old counting, weight, and length are good ones to begin with. How about a graph of some of the world's fish, including the longest and shortest? What are the heaviest and lightest animals? How does a milligram compare with a kilogram? What are all those zeros for, and do I have to write them all out?*

- Arts and Crafts. *What hands-on learner will be able to resist creating her very own geoboard or set of tangrams? How about an exploration of geometric shapes with nothing more than some string and a couple of boxes of straws? Pattern blocks are great inspiration for various projects. To really get your artist going, turn her on to the work of M. C. Escher, a graphic artist known for using patterns in his works. Some of his best known images include those of geese, fish, and hands.*

7 WAYS TO MAKE READING AND WRITING FUN

- Pick a night that fits in your family's schedule and ask everyone to write a letter to someone—a relative, famous person, author, a corporation to criticize or commend a product, or an expert requesting information on a topic of study or interest. Sometimes surprising rewards pop up in the mailbox for the effort.

- Help your child find an e-mail pal who shares an interest.

- Assign character roles from a book you're reading. Act out the roles with different voices, including one for the narrator. Audio or video tape the "performance."

- Read the book before you see the movie. Compare the two.

- If your television is equipped with closed captioning, turn down the sound and "read" TV for a while.

- Have your child read a story on to an audiocassette as a gift for a younger sibling, relative, or neighbor.

- With children's software that makes it easy, have your child create a weekly or bi-weekly newspaper filled with his own "news."

7 Easy Ways to Learn History and Geography

- Hang a map of the United States or the world where it can be easily viewed. Use the map to locate the origin of a letter or phone call.

- Give your child a compass to play with during car trips.

- Spin the globe, pick a country, and then plan an ethnic meal from that country.

- Talk to grandparents, senior citizen neighbors, and friends about their lives.

- Have your child go on the Internet to find a "This Day in History" piece of trivia. Discuss at dinner. Two good sites are www.yahooligans.com/docs/tdih and www.historychannel.com/thisday.

- Let your child quiz *you* on her current history or social studies material.

- Pay attention to the country of origin of items around your home. Keep track and discover which countries make more clothing, electronics, toys, etc. Where are they?

Appendix B
Books, Catalogues,
and Other Sources of Info

BOOKS

Dobson, Linda. *The Ultimate Book of Homeschooling Ideas: 500+ Fun and Creative Learning Activities for Kids Ages 3-12,* Prima Publishing, 2002.

Leebow, Ken. *300 Incredible Things for Kids on the Internet,* 300Incredible.com, LLC, 2001.

Reed, Jean and Donn. *The Home School Source Book,* third edition, Brook Farm Books, 2001.

Rupp, Rebecca. *The Complete Home Learning Source Book,* Three Rivers Press, 1998.

Sharp, Vicki F., et. al. *The Best Web Sites for Teachers,* fifth edition, International Society for Technology in Education (ISTE), 2002.

CATALOGUES

Aristoplay (good quality educational games): 800-634-7738; www.aristoplay.com

Bits and Pieces (an amazing array of puzzles): 800-544-7297; www.bitsandpieces.com

Edmund Scientific Co. (fascinating science stuff): 800-728-6999; www.edsci.com

Greathall Productions (life's best stories told by a master): 800-477-6234; www.greathall.com

F.U.N. Books (an eclectic collection of items for alternative-minded educators): 888-FUN-7020; www.FUN-Books.com

INTERNET

Awesome Library: www.awesomelibrary.org

Big Chalk: www.bigchalk.com

Car Talk's Tom Magliozzi on Education:
   http://cartalk.cars.com/About/ATC/Education/

Chem Comics: www.uky.edu/Projects/Chemcomics/

Easy Fun School: www.easyfunschool.com

Genie U, A Safe Haven for Your Child's Genius:
   www.genieu.com

News You May Have Missed: www.kitchensinkmag.com

Newspapers of the World: www.newspaperlinks.com/home.cfm

Parent Directed Education: www.parentdirectededucation.org

Parent Educator: www.theparenteducator.com

Seymour Papert Essay: www.connectefamily.com/fram4/
   cf0413seymoour/recent_essays/cf0413_cherry-3.html

GUIDES TO TYPICAL CURRICULUM CONTENT

www2.worldbook.com/parents/course_study_curr1.asp

www.kingharvest.com/courseofstudy.html

LOTS OF LEARNING CLOSE TO HOME

Educational supply stores

Internet

Learning centers

Museums and historic sites

National chain office supply stores

Neighbors and friends

Nonprofit organizations

Professionals, who often have brochures, booklets and other information for the asking

Public library

Public radio station

Public television station

Toy stores

Appendix C
Reading List

Armstrong, Thomas. *The Myth of the A.D.D. Child,* Putnam, 1996.

———. *Awakening Your Child's Natural Genius: Enhancing Curiosity, Creativity and Learning Ability,* Tarcher, 1991.

Arons, Stephen. *Compelling Belief: The Culture of American Schooling,* New Press/McGraw-Hill, 1983.

Bloom, Allan. *The Closing of the American Mind,* Simon & Schuster, 1987.

Botstein, Leon. *Jefferson' Children: Education and the Promise of American Culture,* Doubleday, 1997.

Dobson, Linda. *The Homeschooling Book of Answers: The 101 Most Important Questions Answered by Homeschooling's Most Respected Voices,* Prima Publishing, 2002.

Dyer, Dr. Wayne W. *What Do You Really Want for Your Children?,* William Morris, 1985.

Elkind, David. *The Hurried Child: Growing Up Too Fast Too Soon,* Perseus Publishing, 2001.

Gardner, Howard. *Frames of Mind,* Basic Books, 1985.

Gould, Stephen Jay. *The Mismeasure of Man,* W. W. Norton, 1981.

Illich, Ivan. *Deschooling Society,* Harper & Row, 1971.

Kindlon, Daniel J., Michael Thompson, Dan Kindlon. *Raising Cain: Protecting the Emotional Life of Boys,* Ballantine, 2000.

Kohn, Alfie. *Punished By Rewards: The Trouble with Gold Stars, Incentive Plans, A's, Praise, and Other Bribes,* Houghton Mifflin, 1993.

Krishnamurti. *Education and the Significance of Life,* Harper & Row, 1953.

Lewis, Thomas, M.D., Fari Amini, Richard Lannon. *A General Theory of Love,* Vintage Books, 2001.

Leonard, George B. *Education and Ecstasy,* Delacorte Press, 1968.

Michalko, Michael. *Cracking Creativity: The Secrets of Creative Genius,* Ten Speed Press, 2001.

Owen, David. *None of the Above: Behind the Myth of Scholastic Aptitude,* Houghton Mifflin, 1981.

Pipher, Mary. *Reviving Ophelia: Saving the Selves of Adolescent Girls,* Ballantine Books, 2002.

Ratey, John J. *A User's Guide to the Brain: Perception, Attention, and the Four Theaters of the Brain,* Vintage Books, 2002.

Rosenfeld, Alvin, Nicole Wise and Robert Coles. *The Over-Scheduled Child: Avoiding the Hyper-Parenting Trap,* Griffin, 2001.

Schmidt, Laurel. *Seven Times Smarter: 50 Activities, Games, and Projects to Develop the Seven Intelligences of Your Child,* Three Rivers Press, 2001.

Silberman, Charles E. *Crisis in the Classroom,* Random House, 1970.

Smith, Frank. *Insult to Intelligence: The Bureaucratic Invasion of Our Classrooms,* Arbor House, 1986.

Sowell, Thomas. *Inside American Education: The Decline, The Deception, The Dogmas,* The Free Press/Macmillan, 1993.

Van Oech, Roger. *A Whack on the Side of the Head: How You Can Be More Creative,* Warner Books, 1998.

Index